PUZZLES, MAZES AND GAMES

Radha HS is a Bangalore based children's writer. She has written stories, rebus stories, science and craft pieces, games, puzzles and a couple of plays for children of all ages. She has contributed to various Indian and international children's magazines.

Many thanks to my daughter, her friends, their mothers and family members—the patient puzzle testers—they helped by spotting errors, fixing unclear instructions and helped in age-gauging the puzzles.

Published by Scholastic India Pvt. Ltd.
A subsidiary of Scholastic Inc., New York, 10012 (USA).
Publishers since 1920, with international operations in Canada, Australia, New Zealand, the United Kingdom, India, and Hong Kong.

For information regarding permission, write to:
Scholastic India Pvt. Ltd.
Golf View Corporate Tower-A, 3rd Floor,
DLF Phase V, Gurgaon 122002 (India)

First edition: June 2010
Reprinted: July; September; October; December 2010 August; October 2011; February; April August October; December 2012 February 2013
ISBN-13: 978-81-8477-474-0

Printed at Shivam Offset Press, New Delhi

Puzzles, Mazes and Games

Radha H S

SCHOLASTIC
New York Toronto London Auckland
Sydney New Delhi Hong Kong

Duplicate Trays

Which two trays have exactly the same things on them?

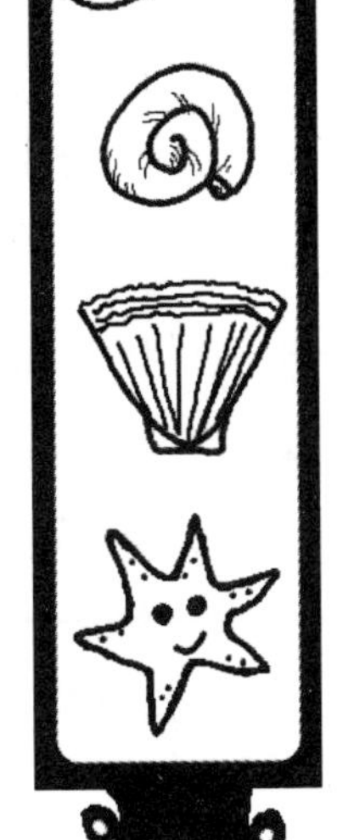

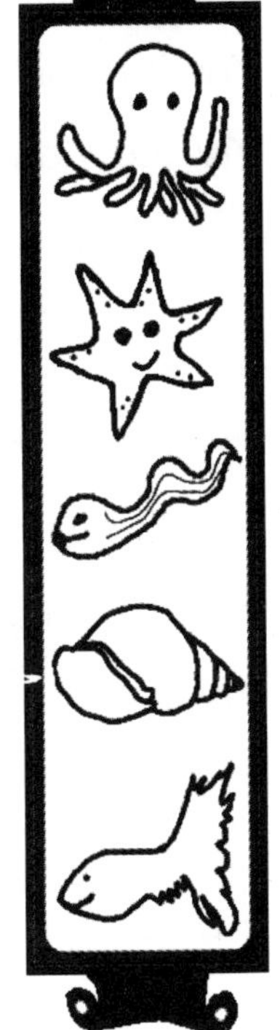

What Am I?

I am big and heavy but still lost in these words. What am I?
One has been done for you.

My first is in egg and also in apple.

My second is in island and also in lovely.

My third is in trace but never in track.

My fourth is in trap and also in plum.

My fifth is in show but never in sow.

My sixth is in track and also in land.

My seventh is in pane and not in ape.

My last is in eight and also in two.

E _ _ _ _ _ _ _ _ _ _

Everyone needs me, but children need me the most. What am I?
One has been done for you.

My first is in five and not in file.

My second is in igloo and also in wind.

My third is in master and also in pit.

My fourth is in bake and also in castor.

My fifth is in moon but not in noon.

My sixth is in slime and also in giddy.

My seventh is in trunk and not in truck.

My last is in snake but never in necklace.

V _ _ _ _ _ _ _ _ _ _

Jumbled Up Sentences

These friends have only ice-cream on their minds and have jumbled up their words. Identify the incorrect word and write the correct one on the blank.

Mahima: I am going to have the biggest chocolate mice-cream ever. ________

Preeti: Can Ramu have a vanilla? He is after all our pet log. ________

Shruti: I am going to have a large banana milk-bake. ________

Gayatri: I love to book at the ice-creams under the glass. ________

Aditya: Okay. While you stare I'll have a fig and honey double soup. ________

Find the Animals

Find the animals and birds listed below in the grid of letters. You can begin at any point and move clockwise or anti-clockwise. The names of the animals will run in the shape of a rectangle or square. The first one has been done for you.

A	S	A	O	E	U	T	Y	E	S	Q
D	F	L	A	R	F	A	G	S	E	P
R	O	E	M	G	A	E	I	A	F	Y
C	G	N	I	F	D	Z	R	A	F	O
U	A	H	P	E	D	A	N	T	A	Z
Y	S	A	K	L	Y	R	R	E	E	O
G	U	N	T	E	S	E	T	A	B	Q
I	Y	D	G	D	W	L	R	E	D	W
H	N	O	C	D	H	F	A	P	M	F
K	I	A	E	S	T	X	N	A	I	E
O	H	S	R	S	T	A	Z	U	H	S
F	R	S	O	E	D	N	E	E	C	J
F	P	G	D	E	R	I	A	O	D	D
U	O	A	L	R	R	E	F	E	E	O
Z	J	Y	L	S	I	A	T	K	E	A
Z	G	S	H	E	E	F	U	G	I	L

1. FLAMINGO
2. GIRAFFES
3. RHINOCEROS
4. CHIMPANZEE
5. REINDEER
6. ANTEATER
7. ELEPHANT

Find the Message

Help Stickman through the maze. Follow the instructions on the boards. At every board you will find two letters. Write these down in the order you find them and then read the entire message as you exit.

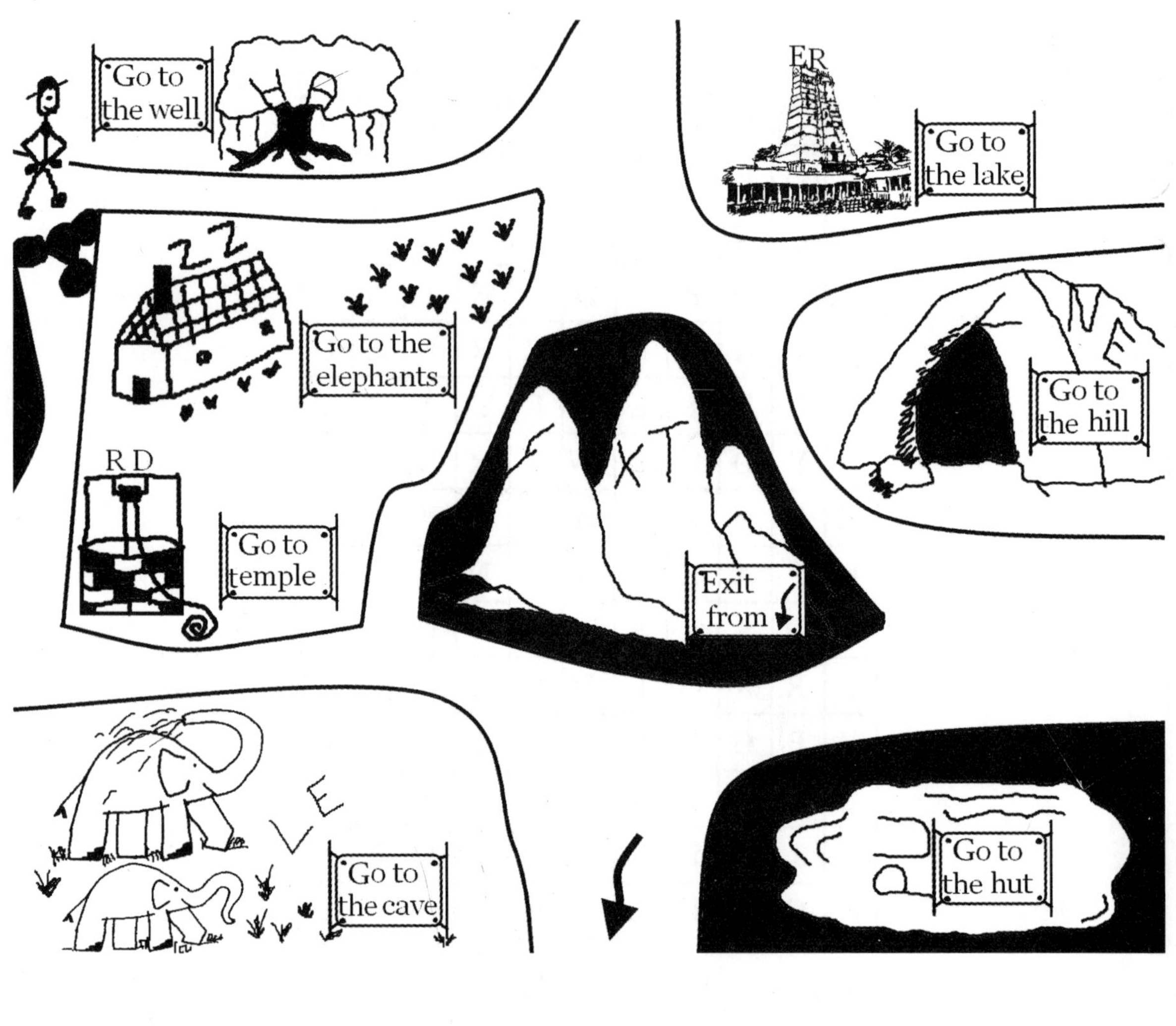

_ TIME!

Follow My Patterns

Follow the patterns on my body to find out why it is a special day for me. Start at the square which is the same pattern as my head (the arrow points to it). Go on to a square right next to the one you are on, which is the same pattern as the next pattern on me. Continue until you come to the tail tip. String the letters together from each of the squares you visit and you will find out why.

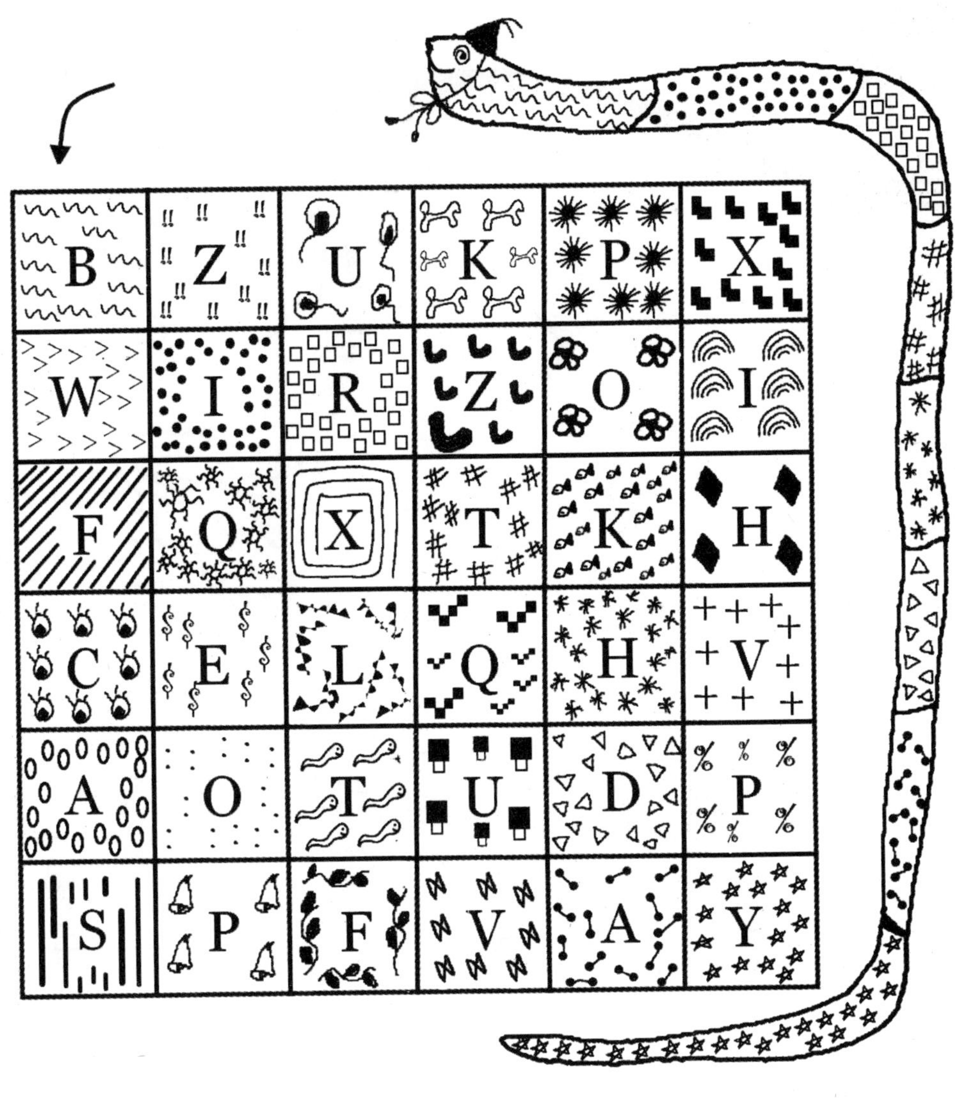

Kite flying Twins

Two twins, Bipasha and Isha, are flying kites with their friends. Theirs are the only kites that are not entangled. Trace the strings to spot the twins.

Letter Galaxy

In the Double Letter Galaxy below, all the words have double letters. These double letters are all flying loose in space. Draw a line from the incomplete word at the centre to the correct double letter, which when put together will make a word. One has been done for you.

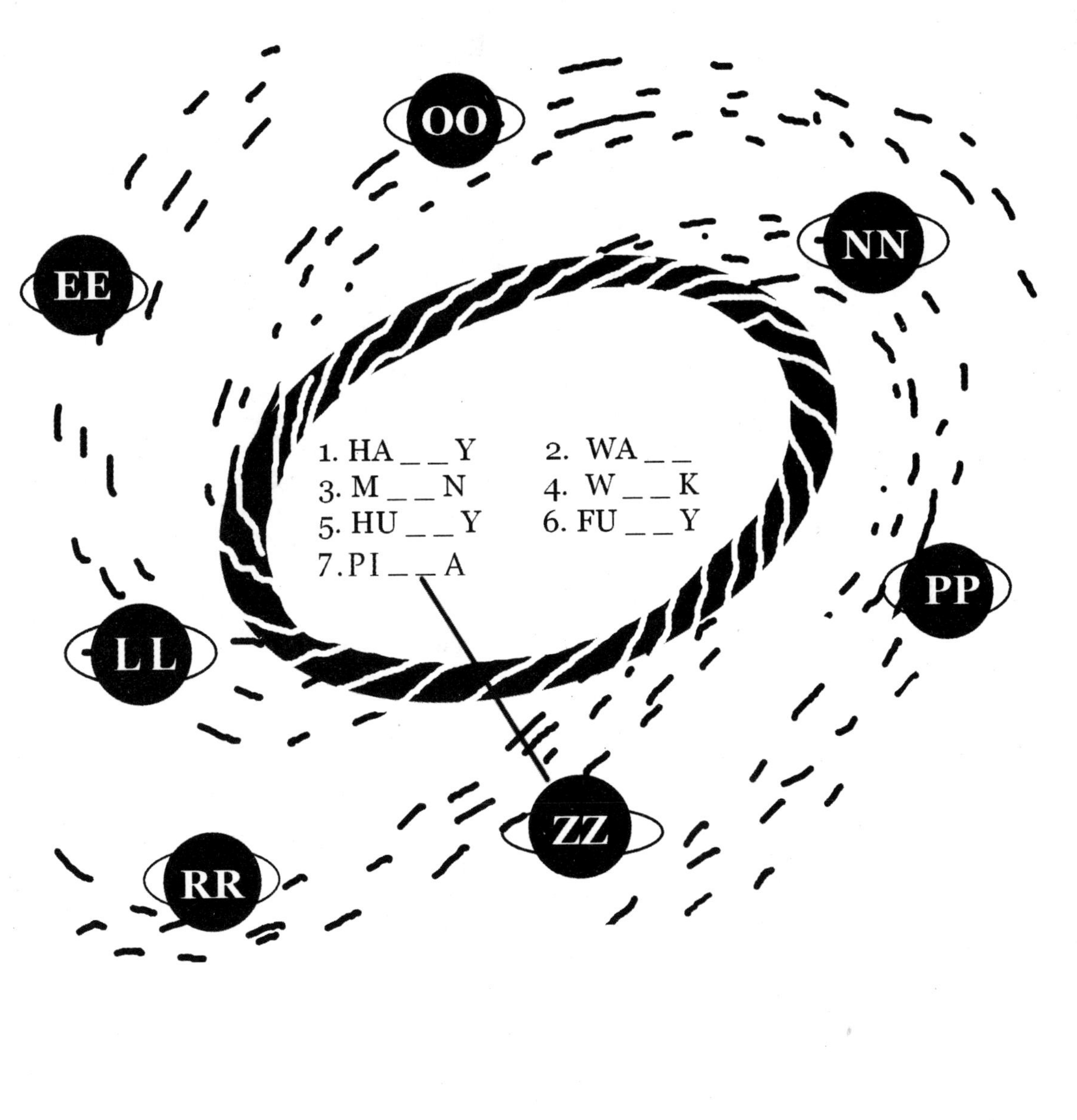

Ice-cream Puzzle

Link the words on the ice-cream sticks with those on the ice-cream pieces to make new, longer words. One has been done for you.

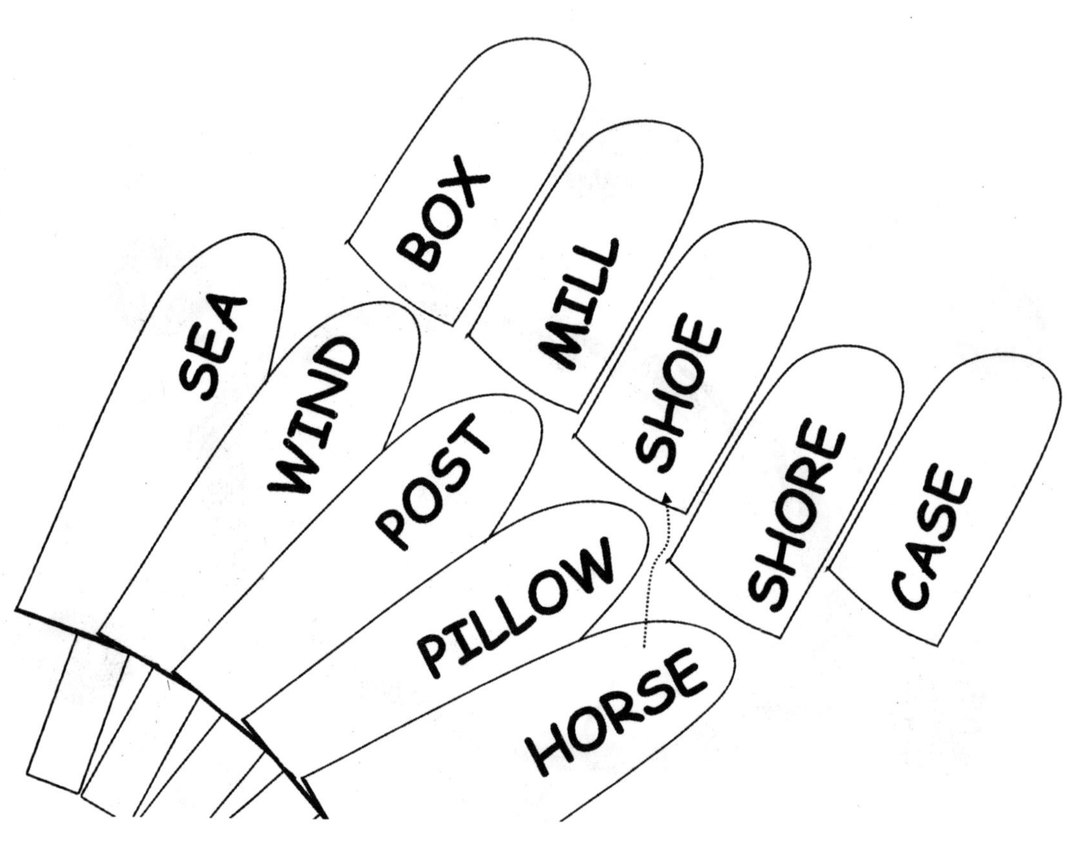

Horseshoe

____

____

____

Lost Animals

These animals are lost. Help them find their homes with the clues.

Donkey: My house is in the shade of a tree.

Mouse: My house is to the west of Donkey's house.

Cat: My house is to the north of Mouse's house.

Dog: I live to the east of Cat's house.

Pig: My house is to the west of Cat's house.

Elephant: I live to the south of Pig's house.

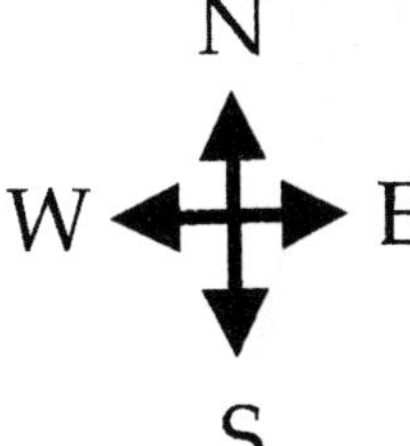

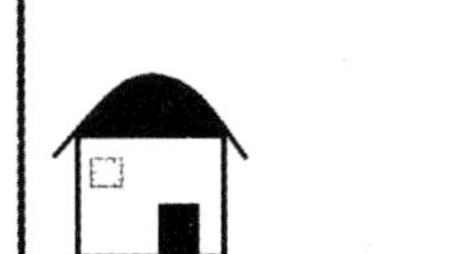

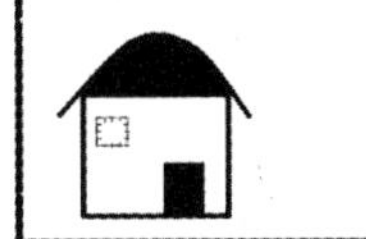

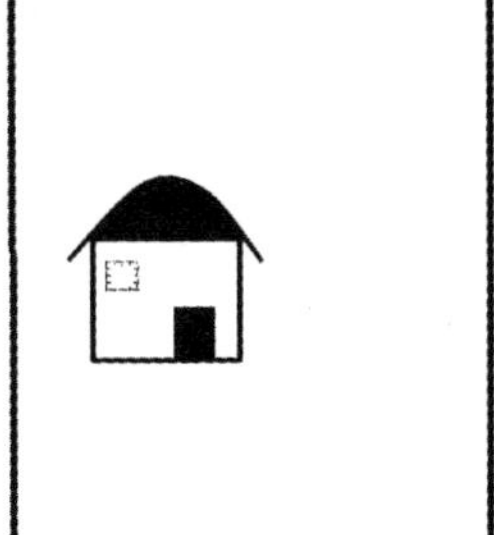

String the Letters

Start at the arrow and string the letters together to make a complete word.

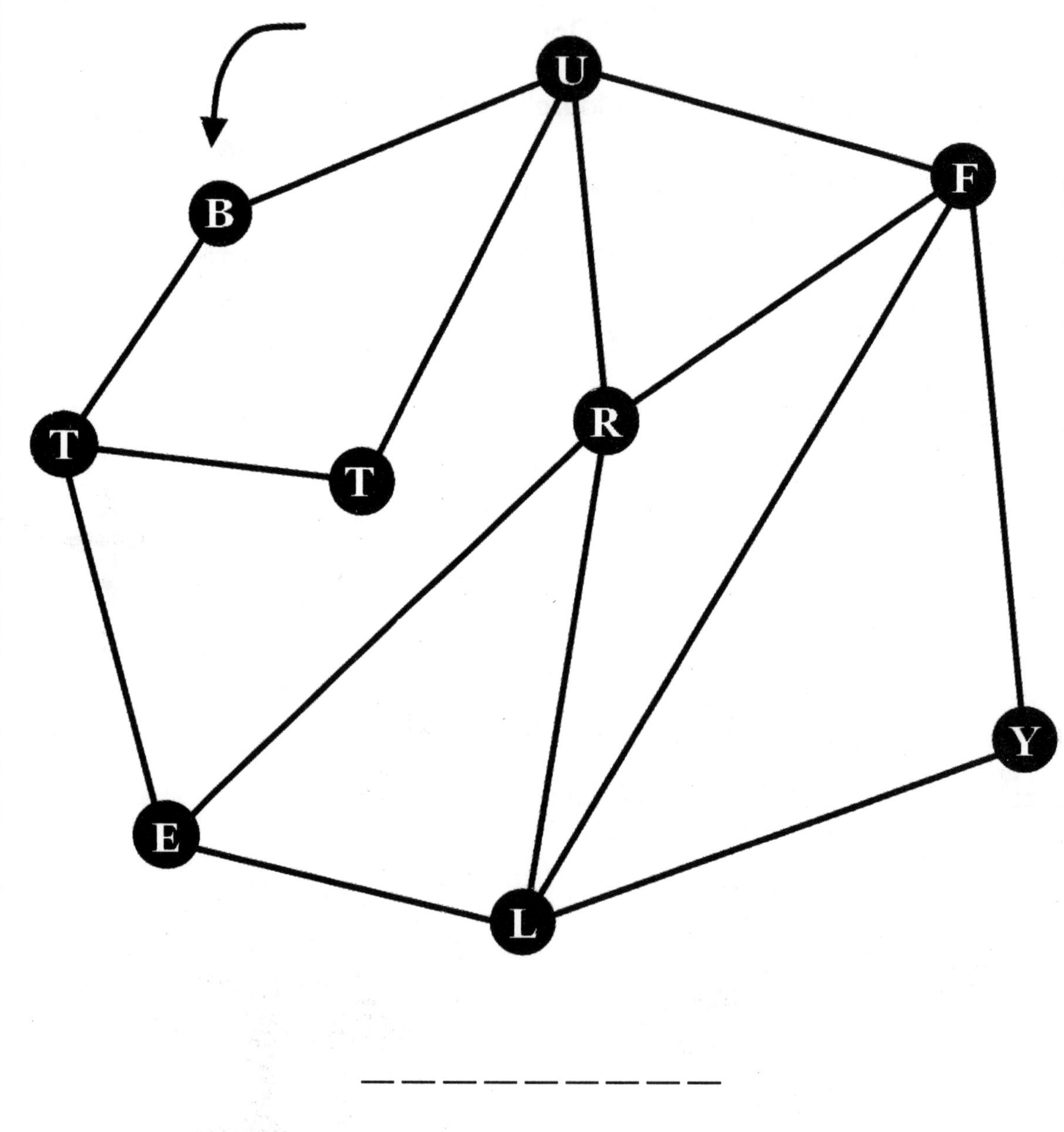

_ _ _ _ _ _ _ _ _

Picture Crossword

Use the picture clues to complete this simple crossword. One word has been filled in for you.

Across

2.

5.

7.

9. 

11. 

Down

1. 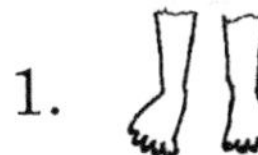

2. 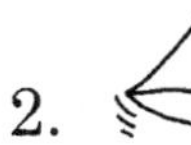

3. 

4. 

6. 

8. 

10. 

11. 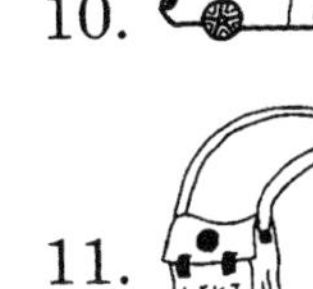

Word within a Word

Each of these creature names have another word hidden within. Can you spot the word? One has been done for you.

BEETLE

BEE

BUTTERFLY

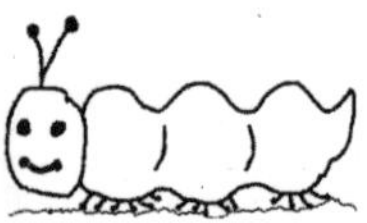

CATERPILLAR

PIGEON

ELEPHANT

Words from a Word

Caterpillar is a long word with whose letters many new words can be formed. How many can you? One has been done for you.

rail, ____________________

____

____

____

Rearrange the Letters

Take the first letter from each of these pictures and rearrange the letters to get something you love to eat on your birthday.

_ _ _ _

Identical Eyes

I am a potato with many eyes, but only five of them are exactly alike. Can you spot them?

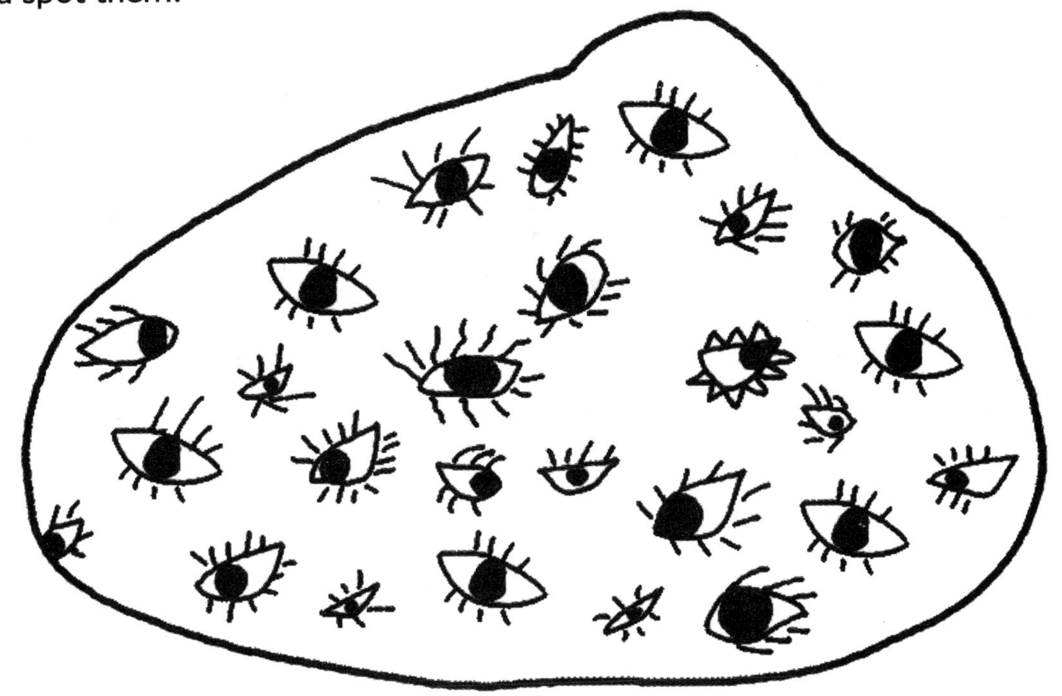

Stolen Puzzle Pieces

Some pieces have been removed from this crossword solution. Can you put in the missing pieces. One has been done for you.

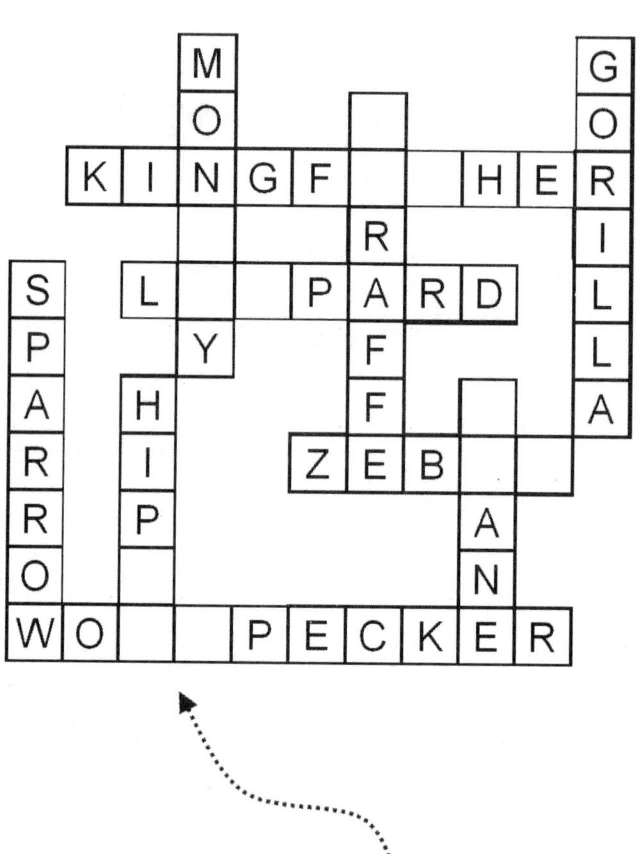

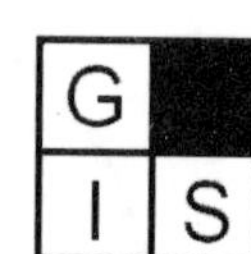

Hungry Snake

This snake is very hungry. Can you spot the dishes that he has eaten? One has been done for you.

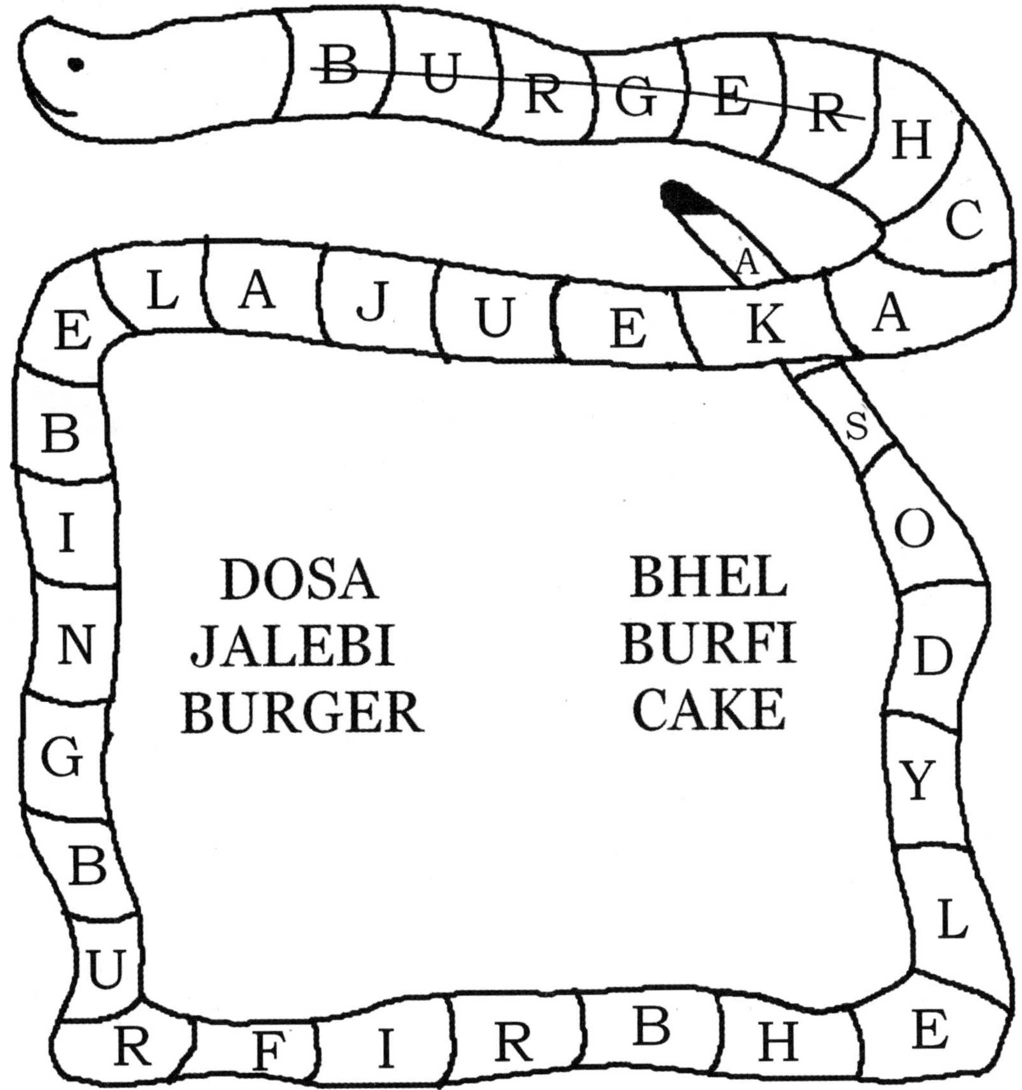

Write down the leftover letters in the order you found them (start at the head and go to the tail) to discover why he ate so much.

_ _ _ _ _ _ _

Confused Bee

The bee at the centre needs to find a path to the edge of the hive. She can only step on numbers that have two digits and whose sum is less than ten.

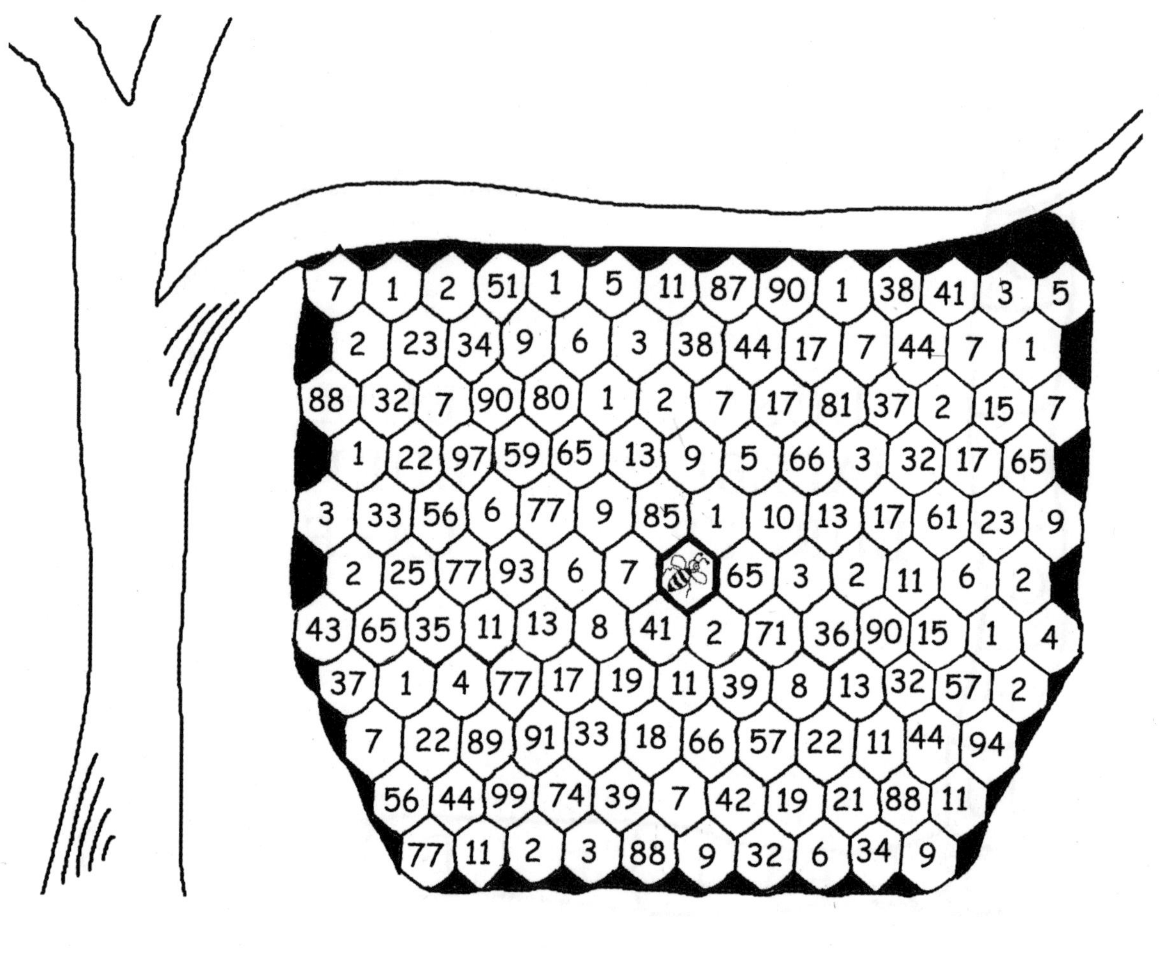

Look Alikes

Two of these figures are exactly alike. Can you spot them?

Spot the Roar

I have lost my roar. Help me find my **roar** among the letters in the grid. My roar appears only once and can run left to right or top to bottom.

Help!

R	A	R	O	R	A	R	O	A	A	R	O
O	R	A	R	O	R	A	O	R	O	A	R
R	A	O	R	A	R	O	R	A	A	R	O
A	O	R	R	A	O	A	A	O	R	A	R
O	A	R	A	R	O	R	A	R	O	A	A
A	R	O	R	A	A	R	O	R	A	O	R
R	O	A	R	O	R	A	R	A	O	R	R
O	R	A	R	O	R	A	O	R	R	A	O

Rope in Pieces

The coiled rope is in several pieces. Count the number of pieces.

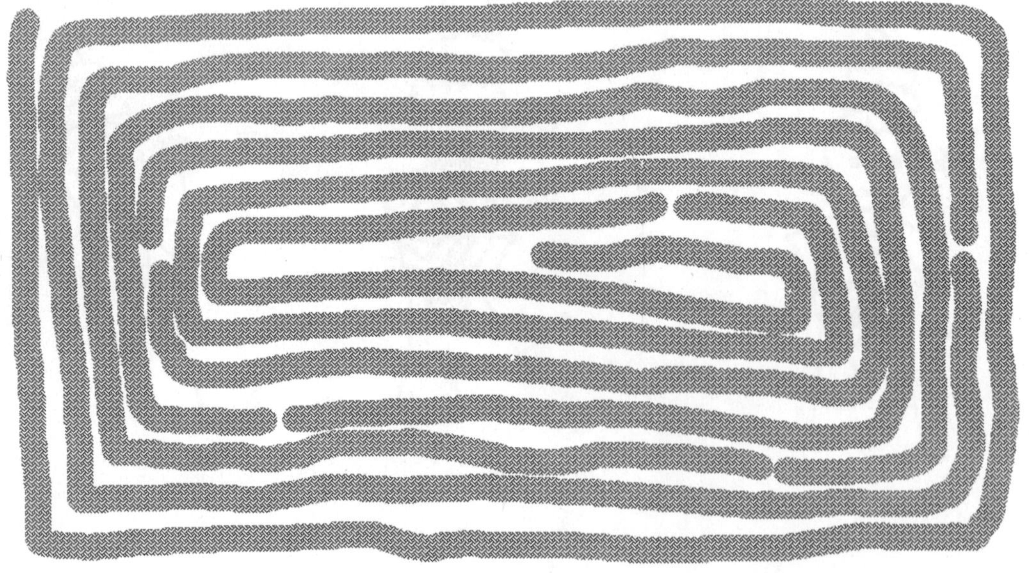

Help the Ant

Help the ant trace a path to her eggs.

Where is the Egg?

Trace the body of the snake to find out if the egg is outside the snake's body or inside it.

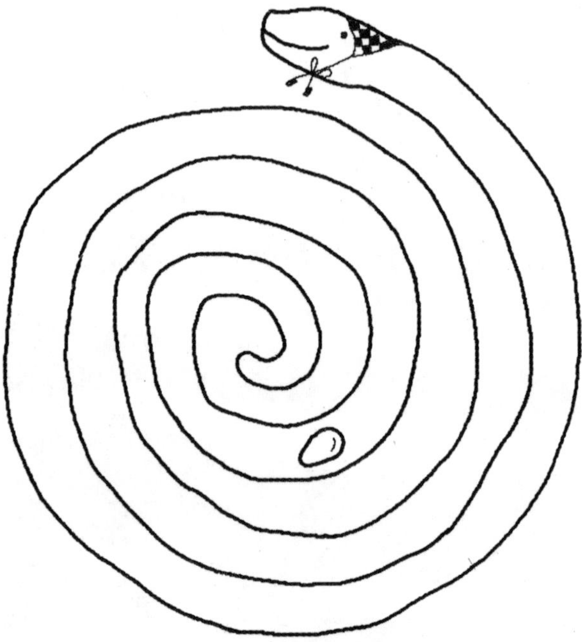

Ant in Trouble

Help the ant remove the leaves, starting with the one on top and moving to the one at the bottom. Write the order in which they are to be removed on the blanks.

____

____

____

____

Cheater's Dice

Identify the dice that do not have the correct markings on them.

Word in Pieces

Put together the pieces to get something you see in the sky.

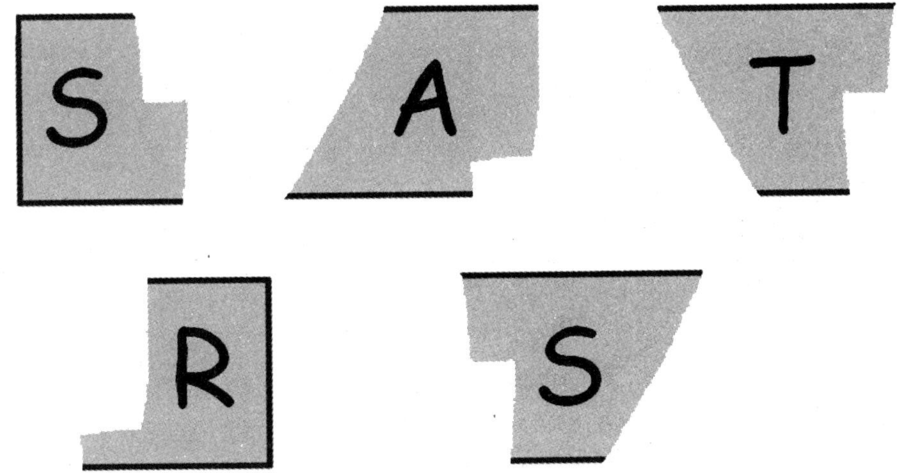

Similar Bunches

Identify the balloon bunches that are identical.

Missing Piece

Find the correct piece (1, 2 or 3) to fill in the missing strip in the picture.

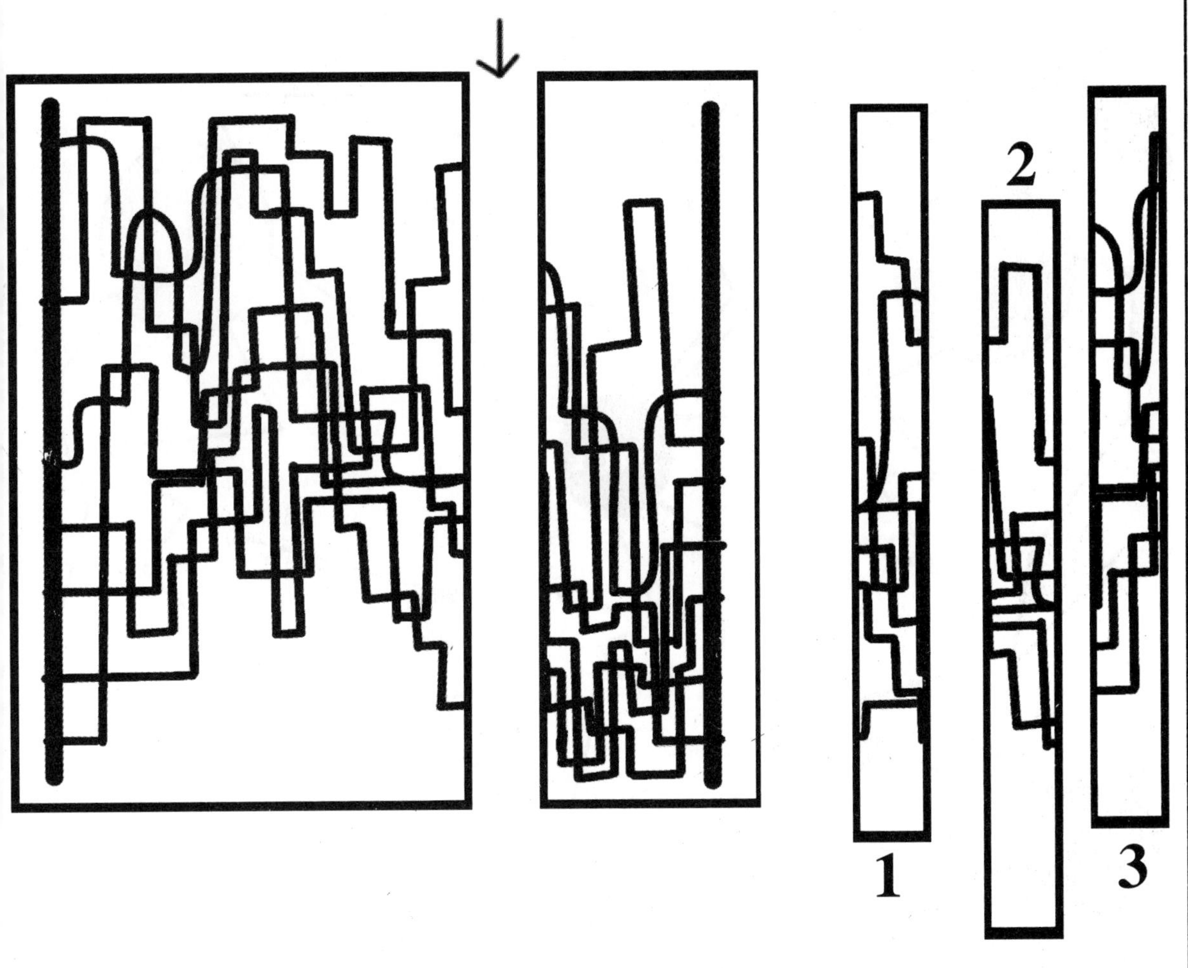

Damaged Flyways

The lines are flyways in space used by people to travel. Some of them were damaged in a storm. Help Stickman the Astronaut spot the flyways with gaps in them.

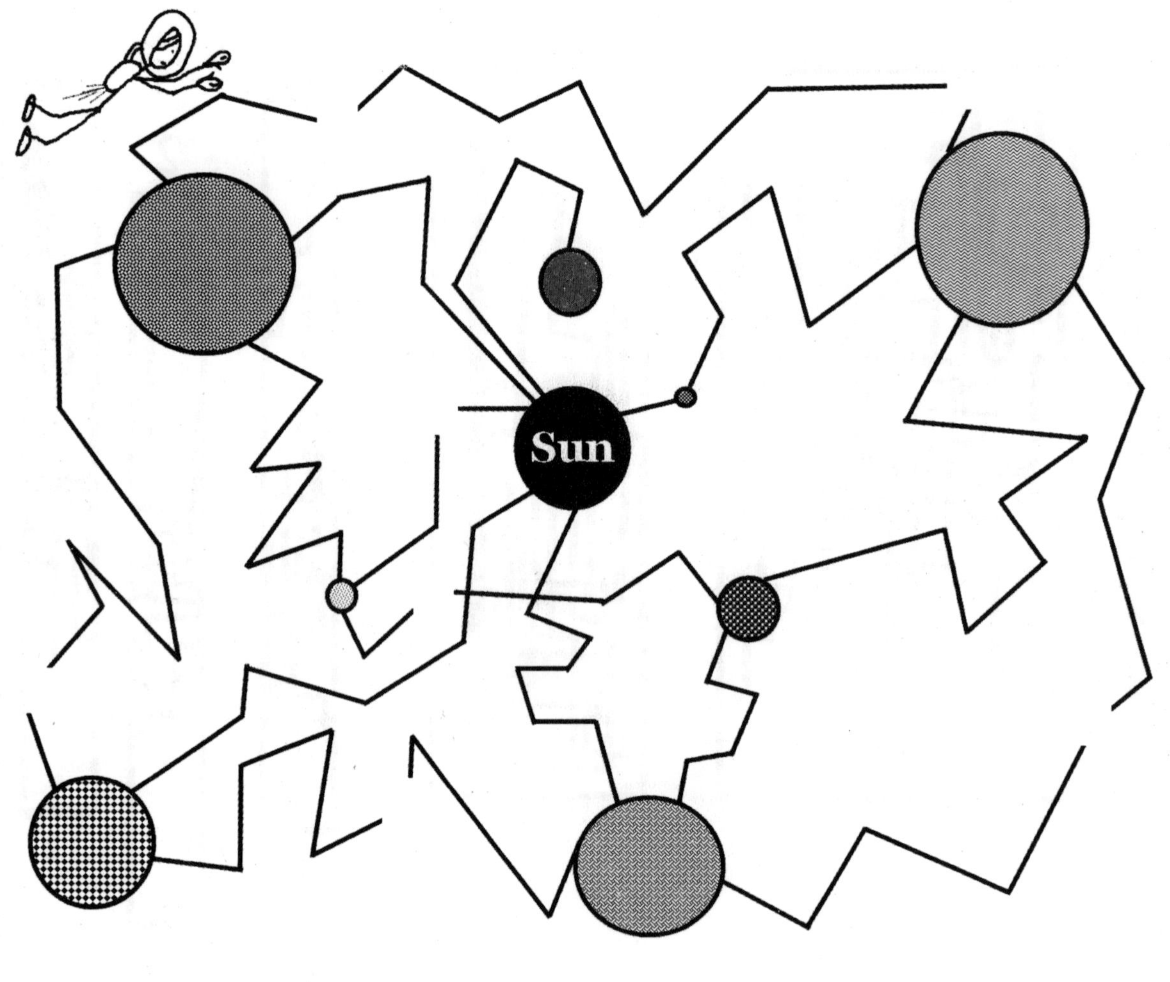

Rebus Pictures

Instruction: Read these words along with the word for the picture. One has been worked out for you. Then try and draw a picture of it in the space next to it. One has been done for you.

MON +  in a  .

Monkey in a hat.

A flying  + PET.

My new 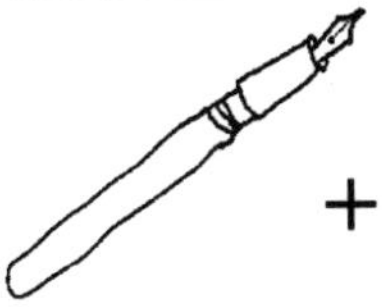 + CIL.

A fat  + ATO.

My P +  have a tear.

I dropped a letter in the POST +  .

Words in a Cube

Rearrange the cubes to form words that can be read left to right and top to bottom. One cube has been placed for you.

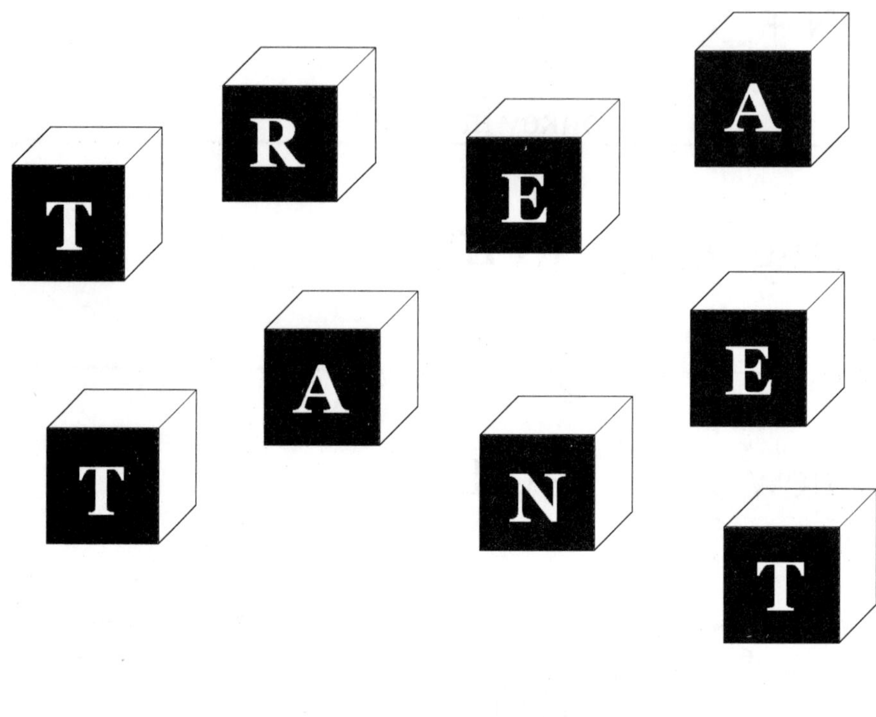

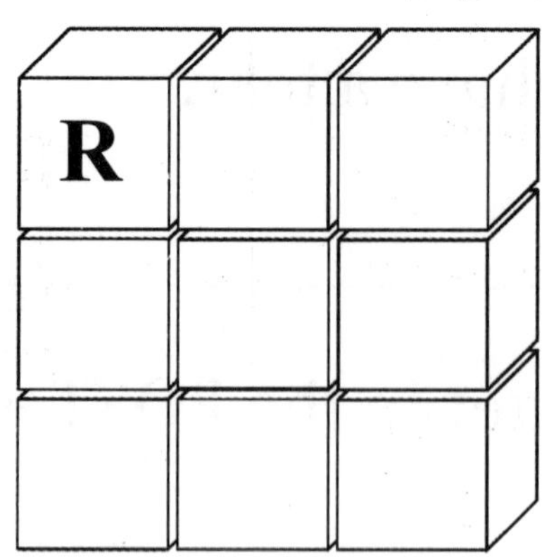

Guess the Letters

Here are some incomplete words. Each group has three words. The first letter has been given in each. The last three letters are common to the three words. Many answers are possible. One has been done for you.

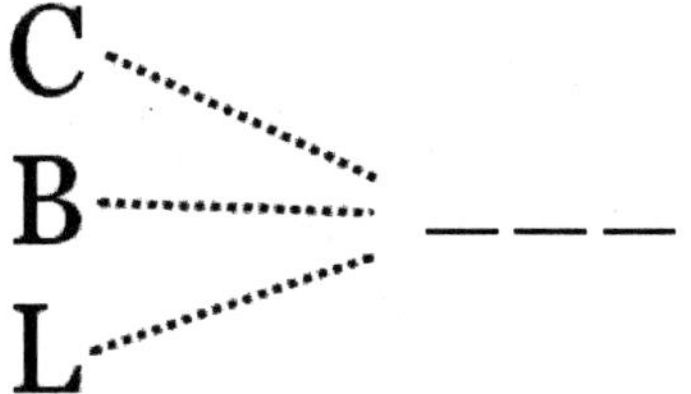

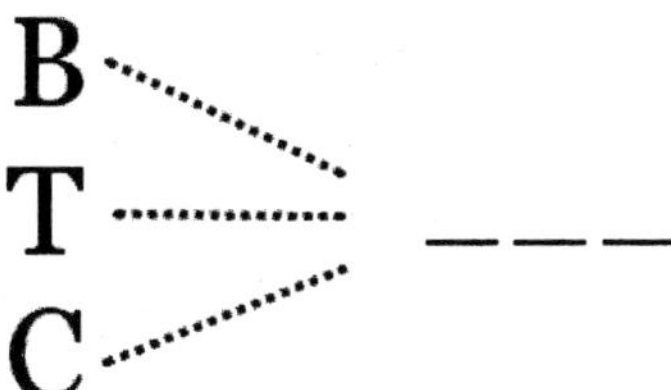

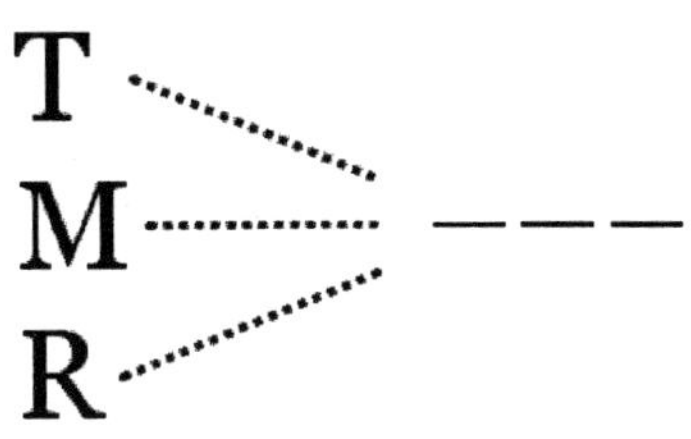

R

S ______

T

Hidden Animals

Six animals are hidden in the grid. Start at any letter and go along the line to the next letter in any direction. One has been done for you.

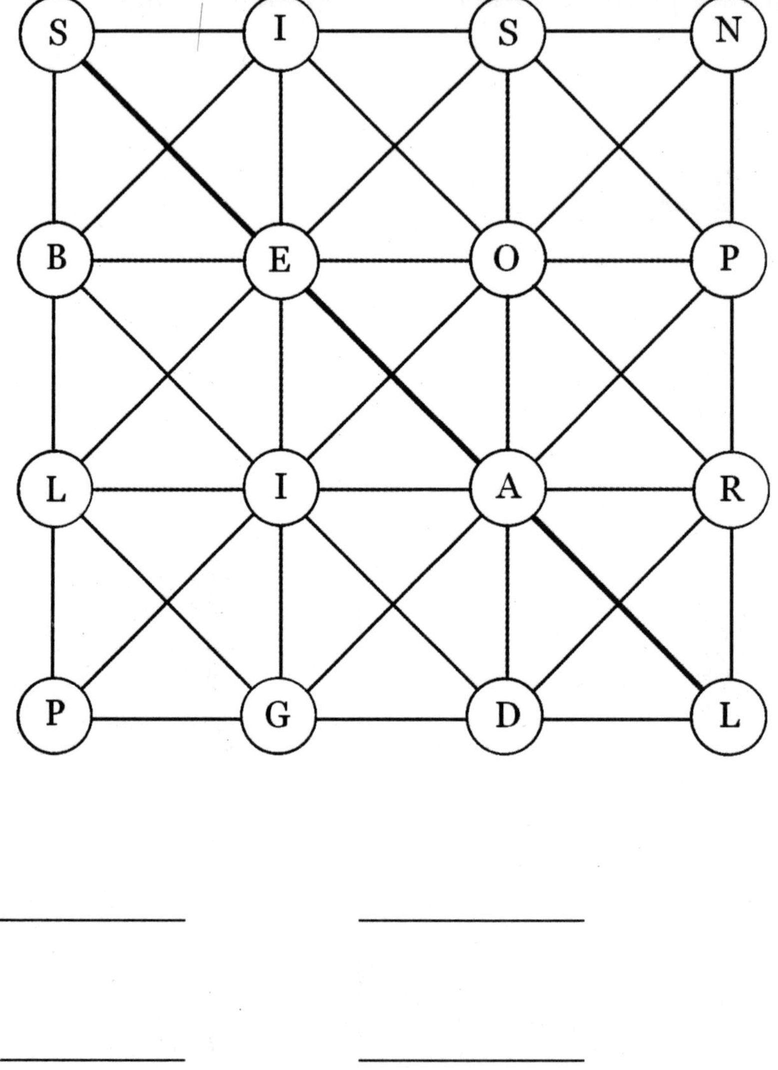

Jungle Race 1

The animals in the jungle had a race one day. They had to start at the big tree and reach the smaller one using the longest route among the flowers. Going over the same route was not allowed. Trace the longest route.

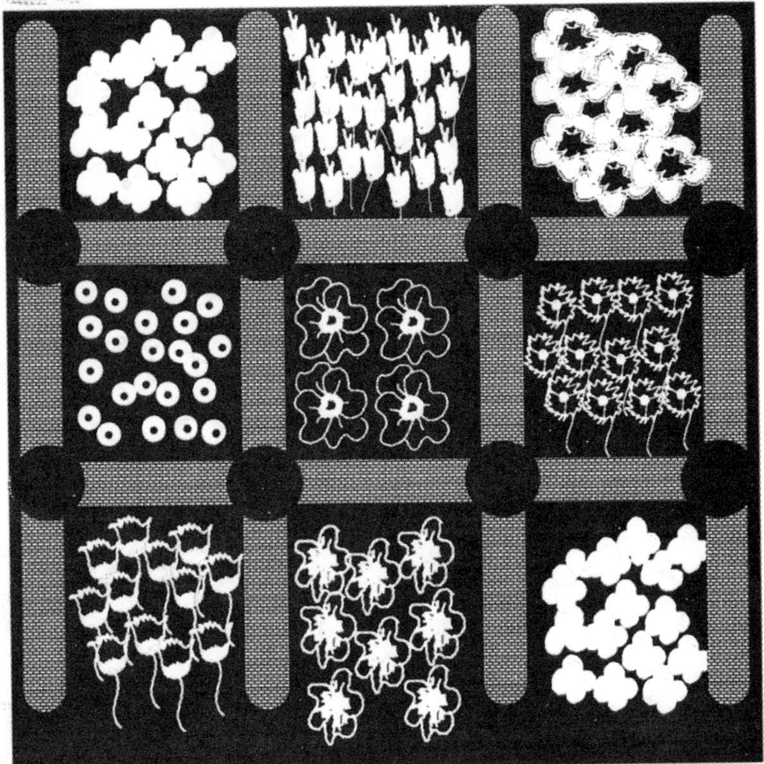

Jungle Race 2

The animal that won the race had as many letters in its name as the length of the winning route. To find the name of the animal go down the honeycomb cells. Start at the top and finish in a cell at the bottom row. You may go down or across, but not up.

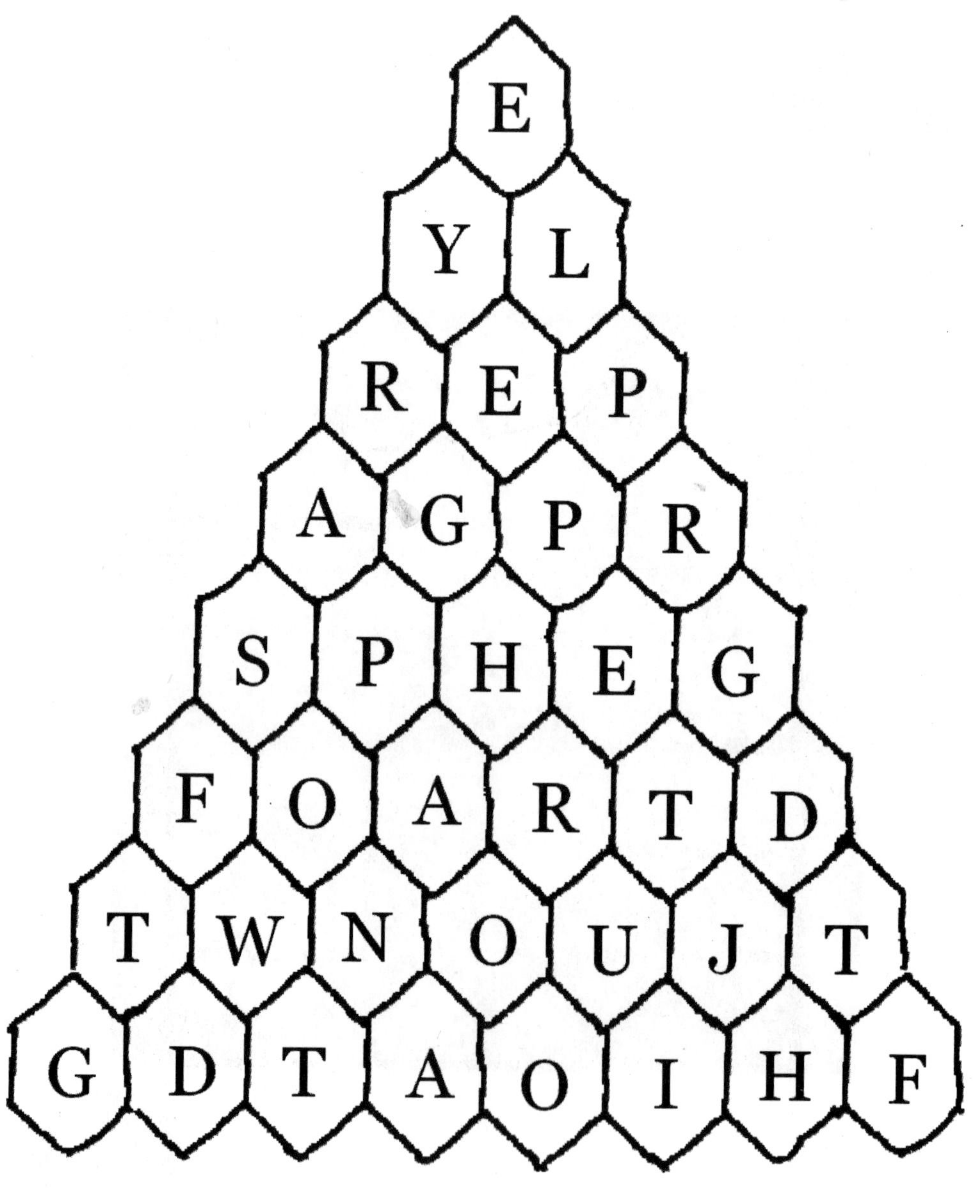

Stickman in the Maze

Help Stickman through the maze to get to his water bottles.

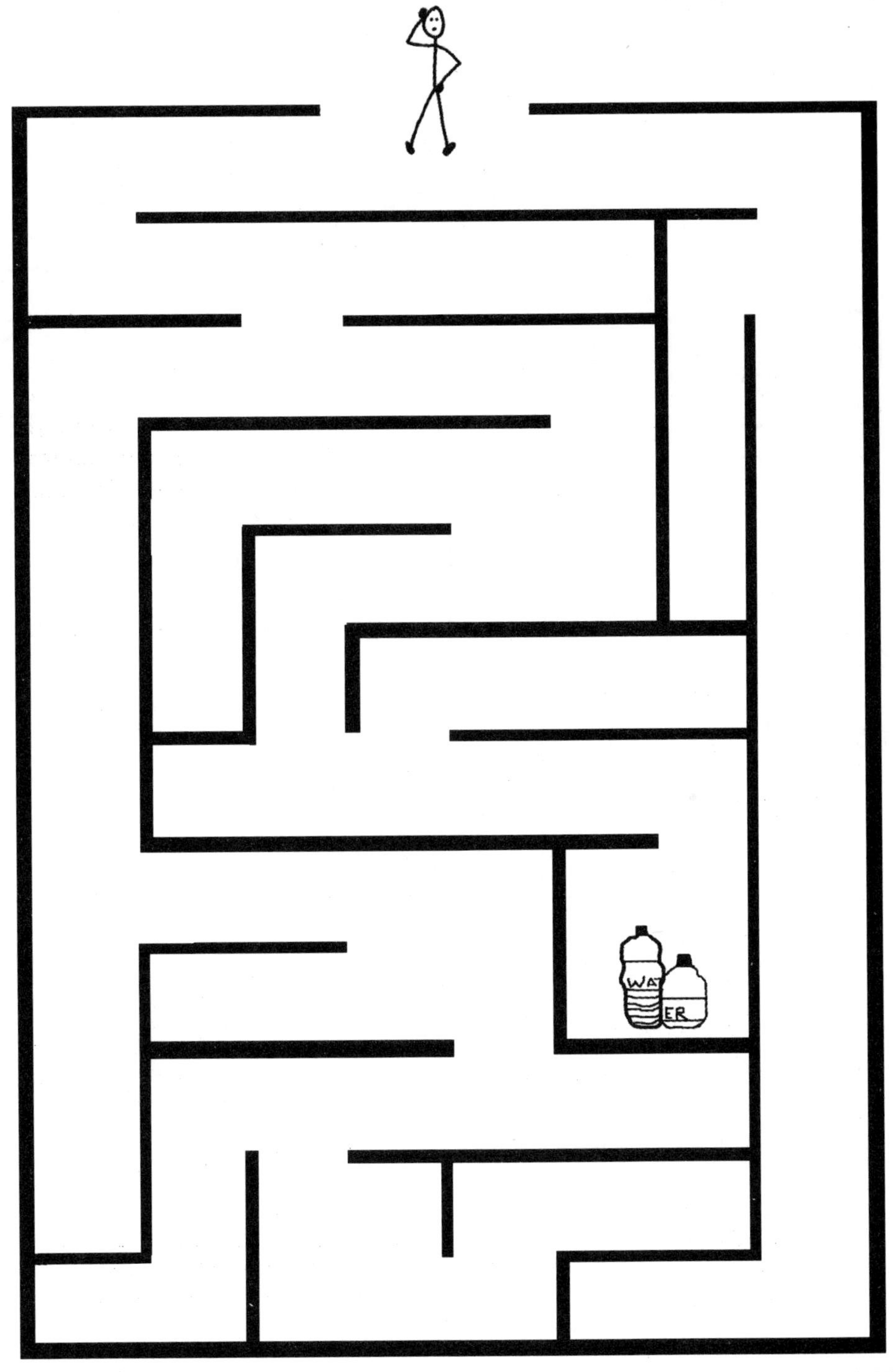

Mystery Flower

The name of a flower is hidden in the trunks. Draw a line from one trunk to another to make the name of the flower. Each trunk can be visited only once.

_ _ _ _ _ _ _ _ _

Hidden Number Names

Each of these sentences has a number name hiding in it. The number name can be divided between two words. Here's an example:
All the puzzles are kept inside the ma**<u>ze</u>** **<u>ro</u>**om. The hidden number name is underlined: ma**<u>ze</u>** **<u>ro</u>**om.

Now try these:

1. She calls herself a sweet woman.
2. The puppy eats even the shoe along with the sock.
3. Be careful when you go near the fire.
4. We stuff our backpacks with books.
5. With great strength reel in the fish.
6. The cat entered the room.
7. We should ban ineffective medicines.
8. What a craze road-skating is!

What's the Letter?

Here is a list of pairs of incomplete words with the first letter missing. Adding the same first letter will complete both words. More than one answer is possible. One has been done for you.

__WIM   **S**WIM
__TUN   **S**TUN

Now try these:

1. __ACK
   __ECK
2. __ING
   __OLL
3. __IRD
   __OND
4. __OLE
   __AIN
5. __ICK
   __ACK
6. __IRE
   __AME

Count and Match

Grandpa bought a few things, but they are all mixed up and so is he!

Did he buy 4 or ?

Help him by counting and matching the things to the numbers given.

Number the Hive

The hive has six letters with six empty cells around each letter. Fill these empty cells with numbers from 1-6 (the numbers 4 and 5 have already been placed). No number can be repeated around a letter. See the sample hive before you begin .

Sample:

Empty hive:

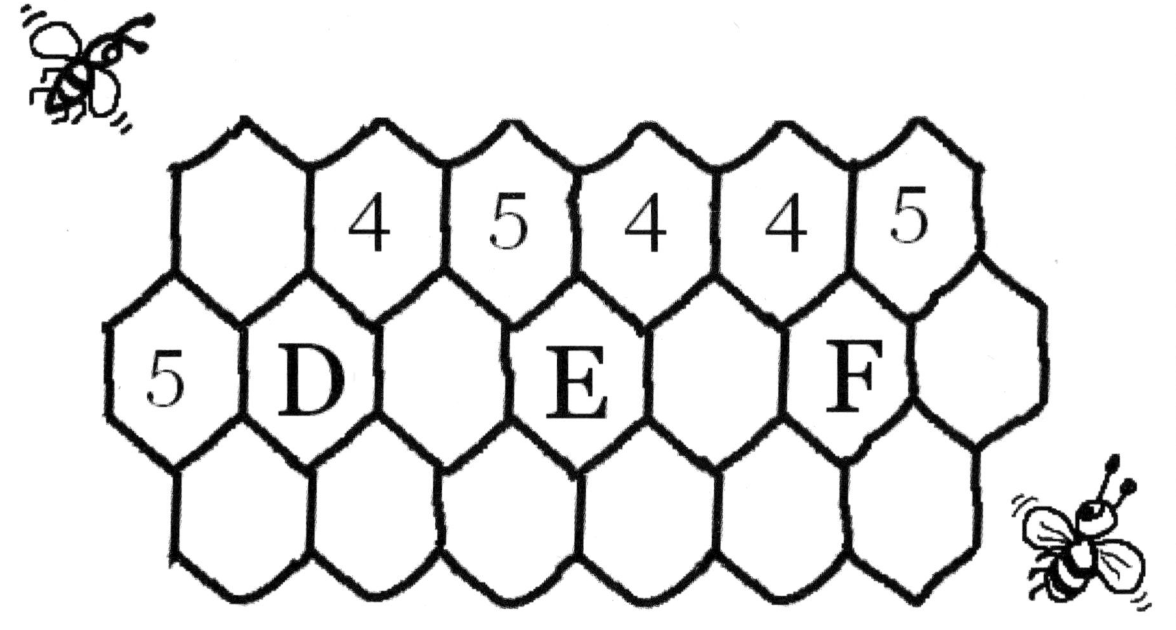

Faded Words

Parts of the words in the box have faded. Help Stickman repaint the words.

____

____

____

____

____

____

Words in a Circle

Fill in the blanks with words that begin and end with the same letter. The number of blanks indicates the number of letters in the word. One has been done for you.

An _ _ _ _ _ can spot its prey while flying high in the sky. (Ans.: e a g l e)

1. I love my __ __ __ and dad.
2. To __ __ __ __ through the keyhole is bad manners.
3. Children love to __ __ __ the balloons at a birthday party.
4. The __ __ __ __ of butter melted quickly on the hot dosas.
5. A lion's __ __ __ __ can be heard far away in a quiet jungle.

Crossword

ACROSS

1 A person who teaches (7)

3 Many children travel on this to school. It's bigger than a car or a van. (3)

5 You hear them from your parents, grandparents or teachers. You can also read them from a book (7)

8 Short form for a dog's young one (3)

10 They are made of paper and you carry them in your bag/backpack to school (5)

12 You light them during Diwali and they have no wax. (5)

13 It's faster than a walk. (3)

14 The day after Sunday (6)

DOWN

1 Piece of furniture you have a meal at (5)

2 A fruit which grows in bunches and can be green, purple, black etc. (6)

4 You go here to study and learn (6)

6 A wild animal, bigger than a bull and very strong, but eats just grass (5)

7 You use this to push in a nail. Ouch, don't hit your thumb! (6)

9 A public place where children go to play. There might be swings and slides. (4)

10 You peel them and eat them. Monkeys too love them (7)

11 What you do when you are happy.

Magician's Maze

Start at the square that the arrow points to and find your way to the square right at the top. There are three types of figures – three, four and five-sided – with numbers within. If the number you step on is even, then the number of sides on the figure should be odd. If the number is odd, then the number of sides on the figure should be even. Keeping this in mind, cross the magician's maze.

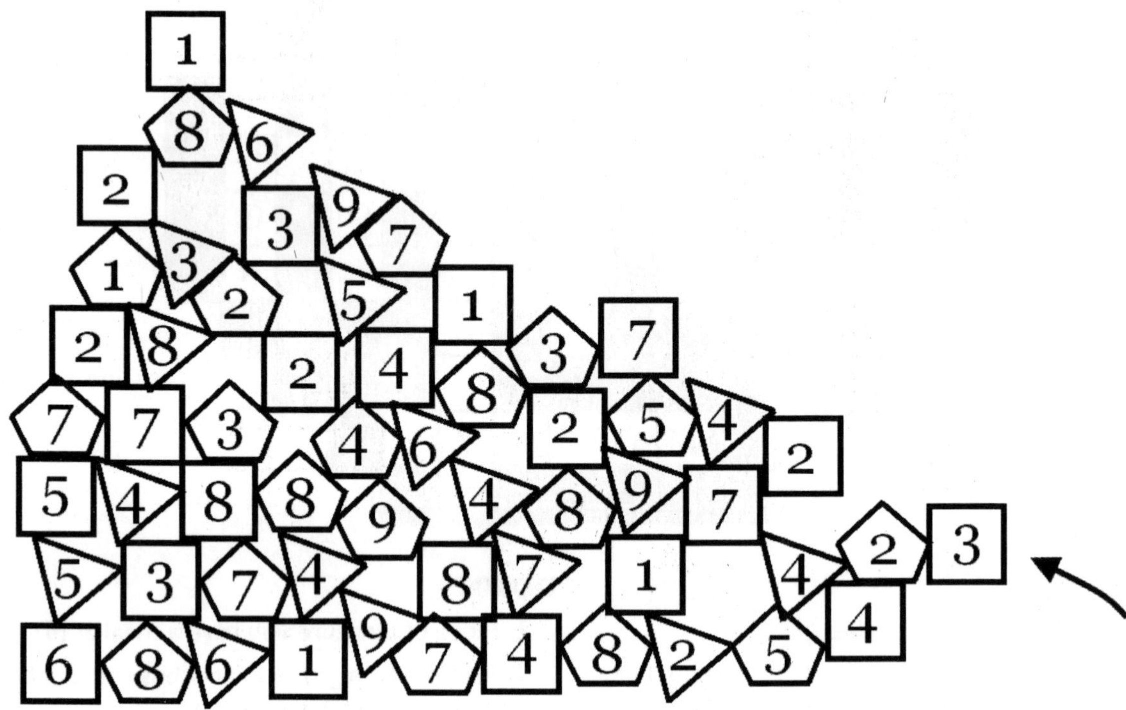

Match the Sounds

Match creatures to the sounds they make by picking the correct options from the two boxes to fill a suitable crossword grid. Creature names run from left to right and sounds from top to bottom. One has been done for you.

donkeys, ducks, mice, elephants, cows, owls, lions, crows

moo, trumpet, bray, squeak, hoot, quack, roar, caw

1.

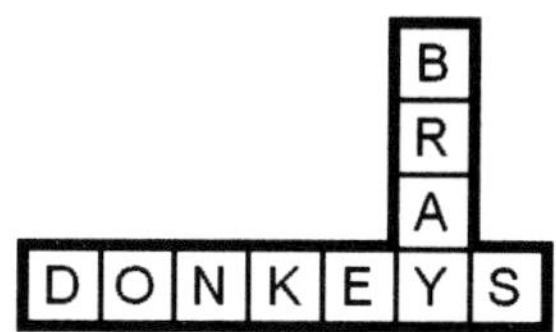

2.

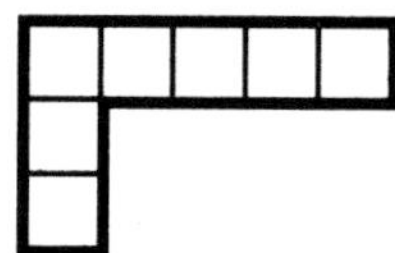

3.

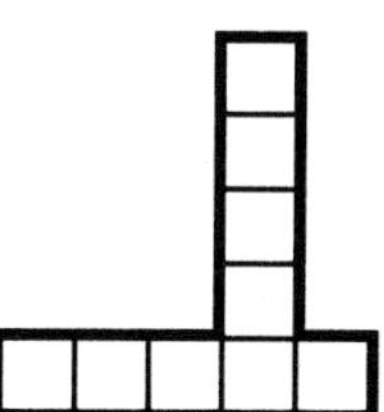

4.

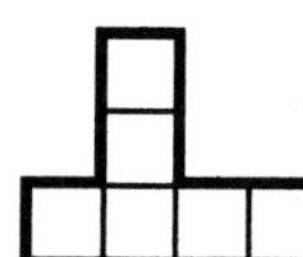

5.

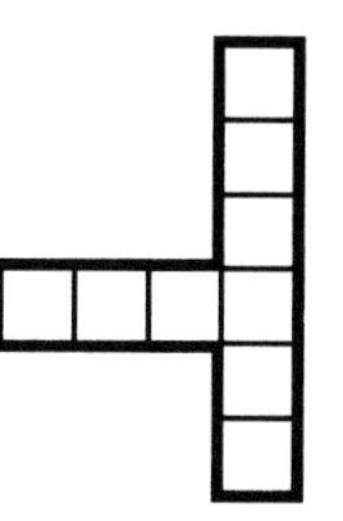

6.

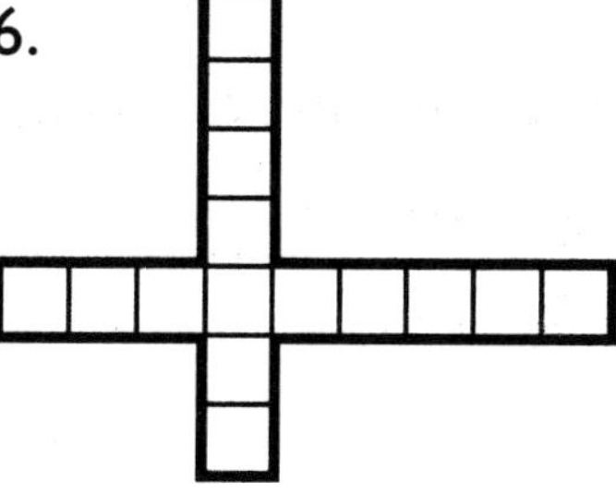

7.

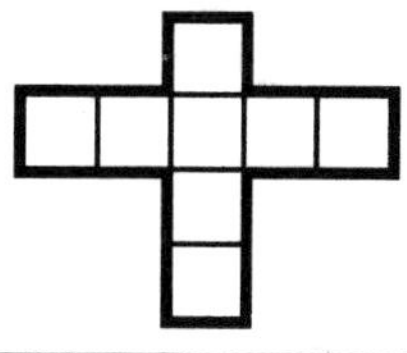

8.

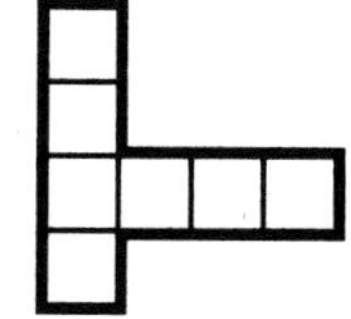

Single Word Squares

Use the clues to fill in the squares. The answer should read the same across and down. One has been done for you.

1 A space between two teeth.

2 'When they wanted to know my ___ ___ ___ ,
I said I was six years old.'

3 A clothes clip is also called a '___ ___ ___'.

G	A	P
A	G	E
P	E	G

A.

1 Opposite of 'good'.

2 Chimp, gorilla and orangutan are examples of this.

3 A lion's home.

B.

1 Our ___ ___ ___ ___ was to visit my grandparents at the end.

2 With a ruler one can draw a straight ___ ___ ___ ___.

3 There were ___ ___ ___ ___ all over the sugar bowl.

4 A bird's home.

Lost Pictures

In this mixed-up picture crossword, the solution and the picture clues have been given, but the clue numbers are missing. Number the clues by matching the word to the picture. One has been done for you.

ANSWERS

Page 5; Duplicate Trays

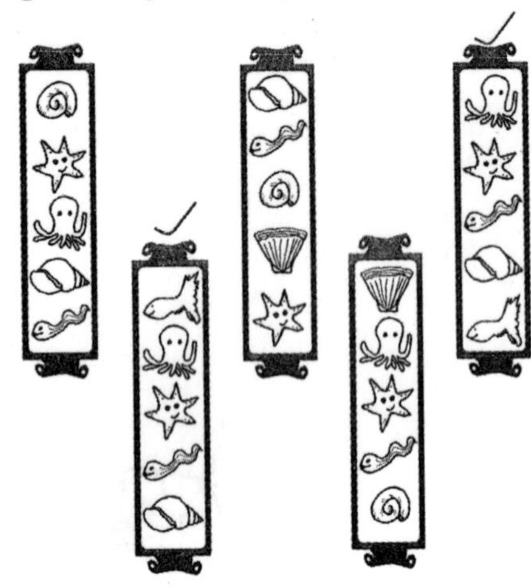

Page 6; What Am I?

1. ELEPHANT 2. VITAMINS

Page 6; Jumbled up Sentences

Mahima: I am going to have the biggest chocolate *mice-cream* ever. It's **ice-cream**.
Preeti: Can Ramu have a vanilla? He is after all our pet *log*. It's **dog**.
Shruti: I am going to have a large banana *milk-bake*. It's **milk-shake**.
Gayatri: I love to *book* at the ice-creams under the glass. It's **look**.
Aditya: Okay. While you stare I'll have a fig and honey double *soup*. It's **scoop**.

Page 7; Find the Animals

A	S	A	O	E	U	T	Y	E	S	Q
D	F	L	A	R	F	A	G	S	E	P
R	O	E	M	G	A	E	I	A	F	Y
C	G	N	I	F	D	Z	R	A	F	O
U	A	H	P	E	D	A	N	T	A	Z
Y	S	A	K	L	Y	R	R	E	E	O
G	U	N	T	E	S	E	T	A	B	Q
I	Y	D	G	D	W	L	R	E	D	W
H	N	O	C	D	H	F	A	P	M	F
K	I	A	E	S	T	X	N	A	I	E
O	H	S	R	S	T	A	Z	U	H	S
F	R	S	O	E	D	N	E	E	C	J
F	P	G	D	E	R	I	A	O	D	D
U	O	A	L	R	R	E	F	E	E	O
Z	J	Y	L	S	I	A	T	K	E	A
Z	G	S	H	E	E	F	U	G	I	L

Page 8; Find the Message

HARDER PUZZLE NEXT TIME!

Page 9; Follow my Patterns

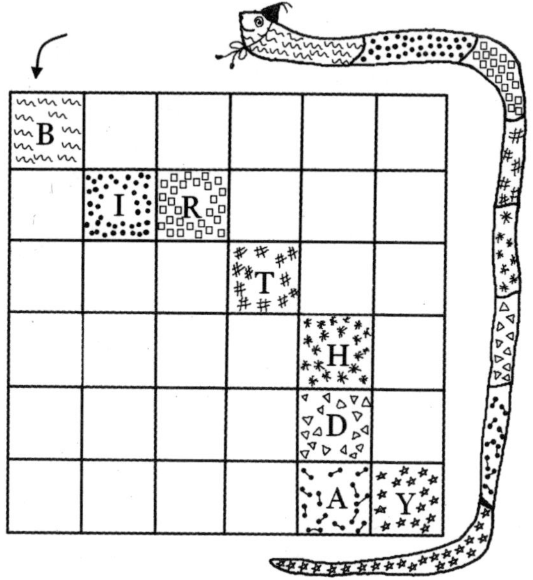

Page 12; Ice-cream Puzzle

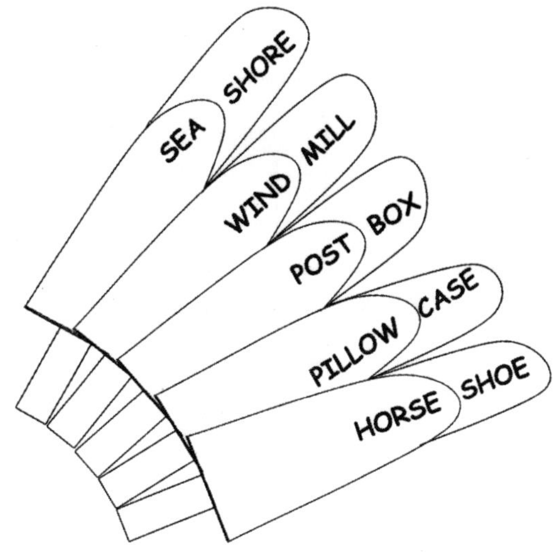

Page 13; Lost Animals

Page 10; Kite Flying Twins

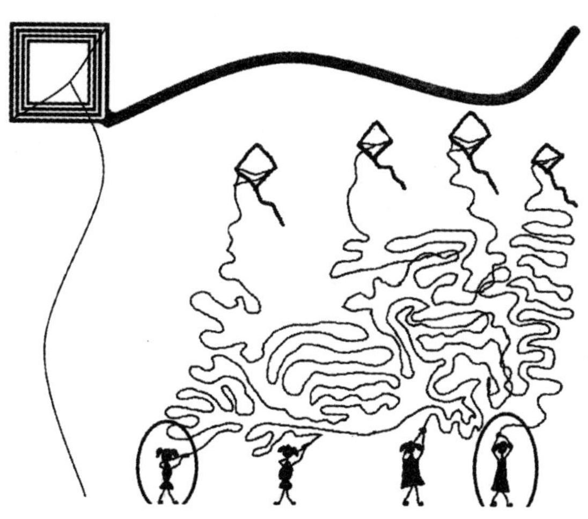

Page 14; String the Letters

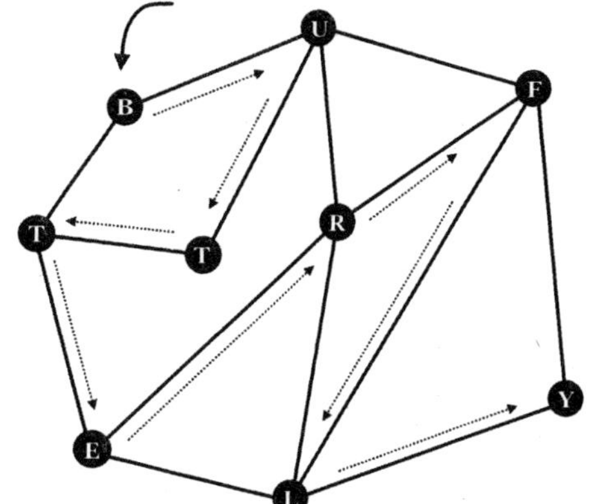

Page 11; Letter Galaxy

1. HAPPY 2. WALL
3. MOON 4. WEEK
5. HURRY 6. FUNNY

Page 15; Picture Crossword

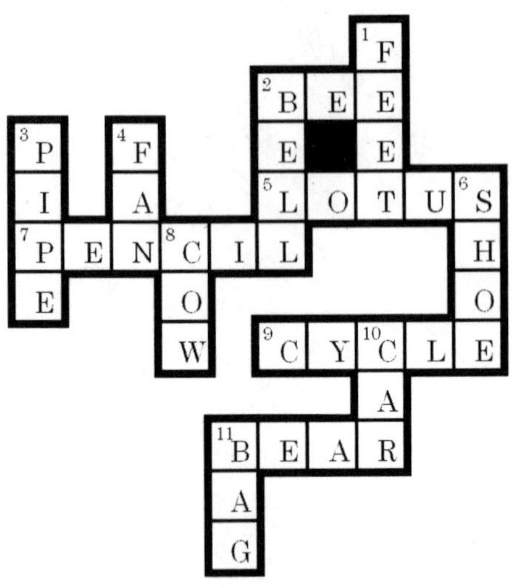

Page 17; Rearrange the Letters

Page 16; Word within a Word

Page 17; Identical Eyes

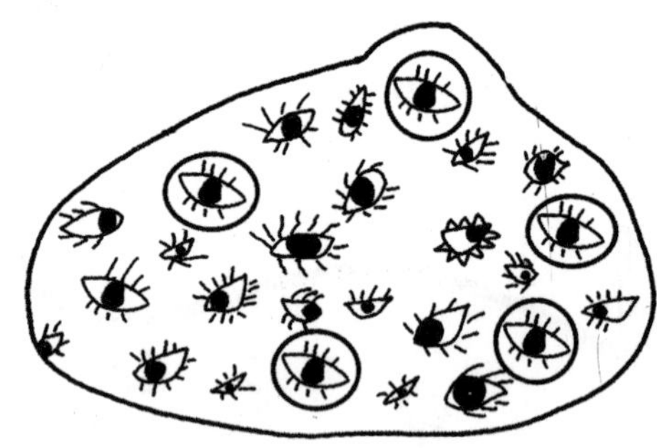

Page 16; Words from a Word

Here are a few….rail, pail, tail, ail, pill, till, lip, rip, tip, pit, lit, cat, pat, rat, tar, art, lair, liar, tear, pair, pear, read, trip, par, rap, lap, trill, tape, ape, pea, pile, rile, tile, car.

Page 18; Stolen Puzzle Pieces

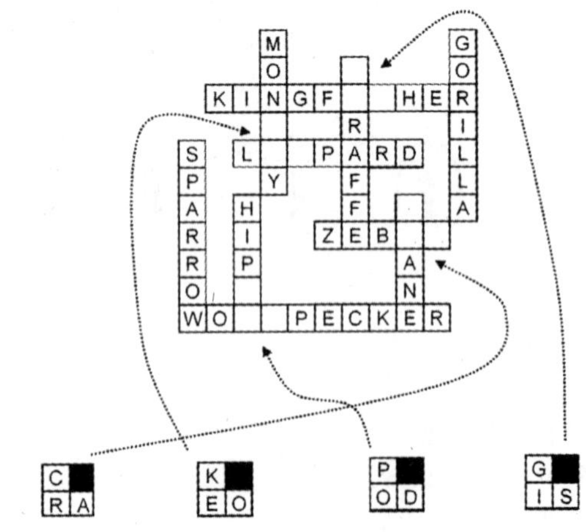

Page 19; Hungry Snake

Page 20; Confused Bee

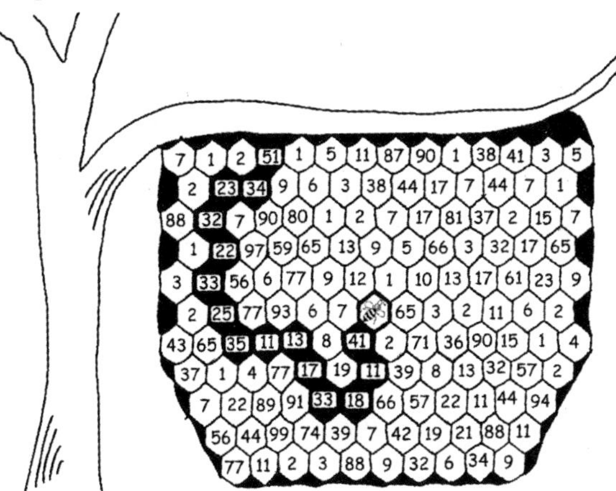

Page 21; Look Alikes

Page 22; Spot the Roar

R	A	R	O	R	A	R	O	A	A	R	O
O	R	A	R	O	R	A	O	R	O	A	R
R	A	O	R	A	R	O	R	A	A	R	O
A	O	R	R	A	O	A	A	O	R	A	R
O	A	R	A	R	O	R	A	R	O	A	A
A	R	O	R	A	A	R	O	R	A	O	R
R	O	A	R	O	R	A	R	A	O	R	R
O	R	A	R	O	R	A	O	R	R	A	O

Page 22; Rope in Pieces

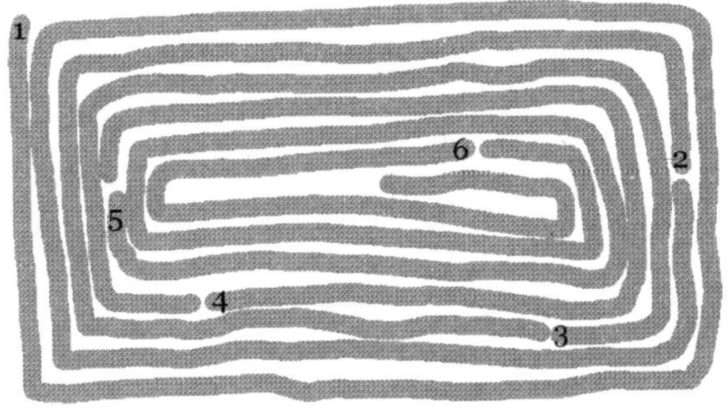

Page 23; Help the Ant

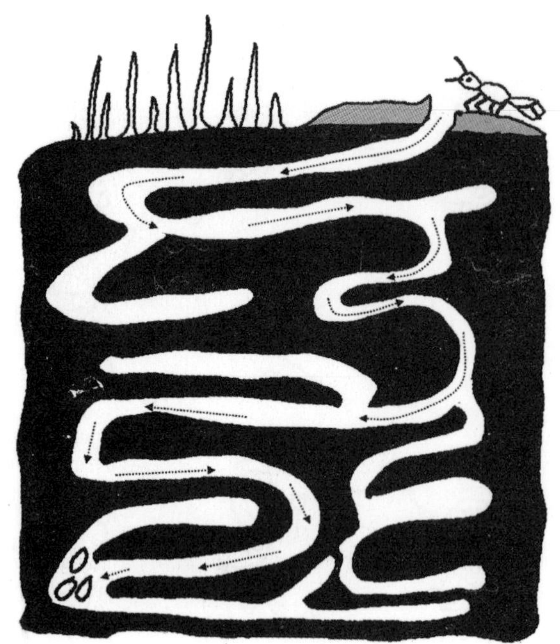

Page 24; Where is the Egg?
It's outside the snake.

Page 24; Ant in Trouble
The leaves are to be removed in this order: 3, 4, 1, 2

Page 25; Cheater's Dice

Page 25; Word in Pieces

Page 26; Similar Bunches

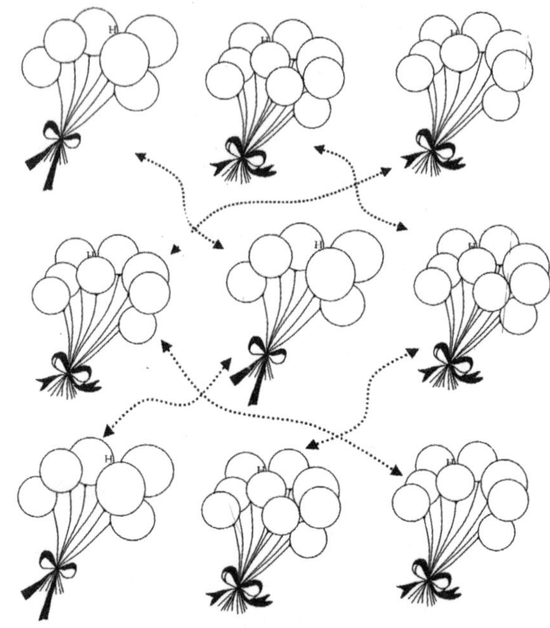

Page 27; Missing Piece

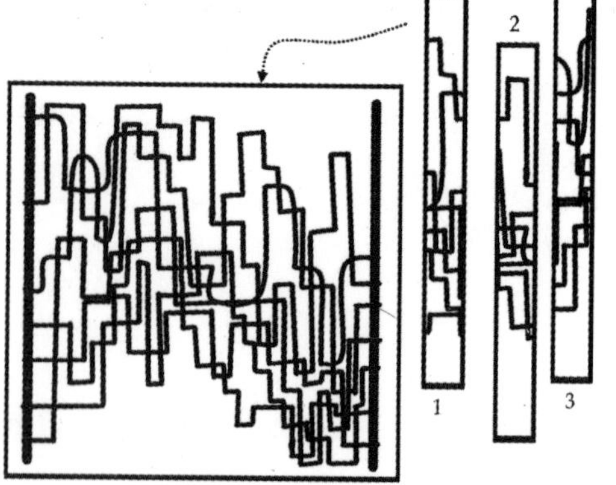

Page 28; Damaged Flyways

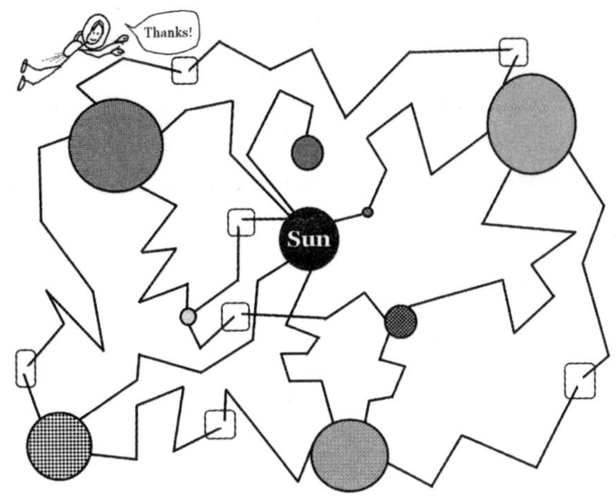

Page 29; Rebus Pictures

MON + in a

Monkey in a hat.

A flying + PET.

A flying carpet.

My new + CIL.

My new pencil.

A fat + ATO.

A fat potato.

My P + have a tear.

My pants have a tear.

I dropped a letter in the POST + .

I dropped a letter in the postbox.

Page 30; Words in a Cube

Page 31; Guess the Letters

Cake, Bake, Lake
Tail, Mail, Rail

Bone, Tone, Cone
Ride, Side, Tide

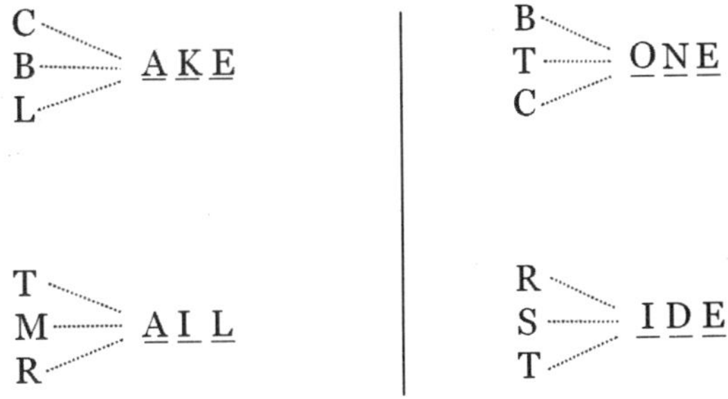

Page 32; Hidden Animals

SEAL, LEOPARD, BEAR, PIG, BISON, LION

Page 33; Jungle Race 1

Longest length – 8.

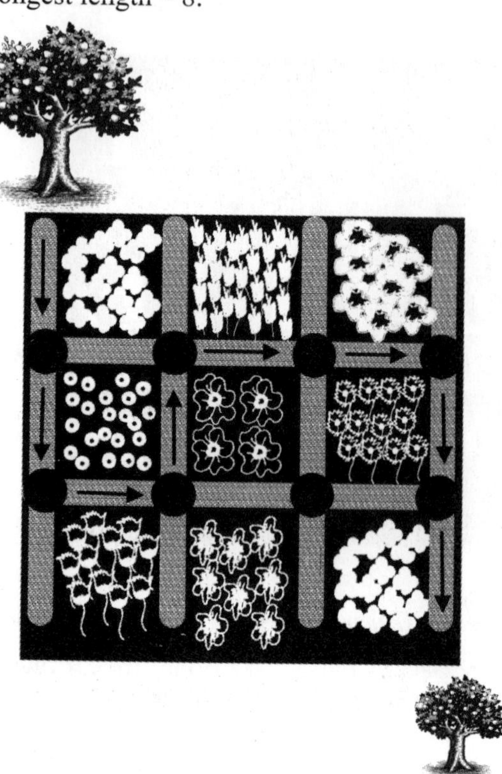

Page 34; Jungle Race 2

The animal that won the race was the elephant

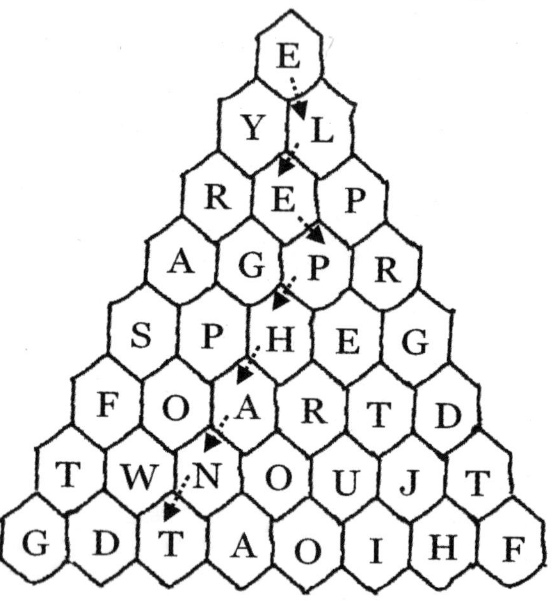

Page 35; Stickman in the Maze

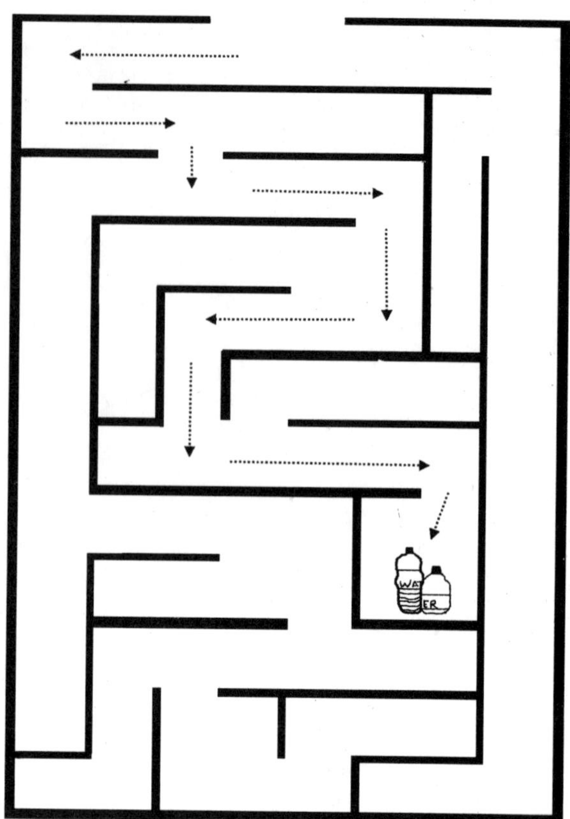

Page 36; Mystery Flower

One suggested path. There can be others.

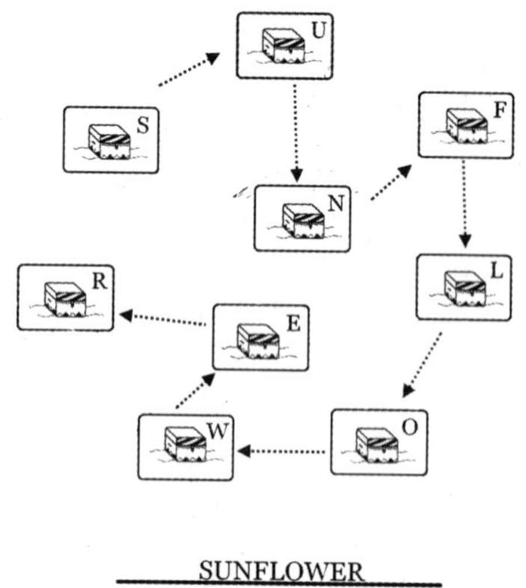

Page 37; Hidden Number Names

1. She calls herself a sweet **wo**man.
2. The puppy pull**s** **even** the shoe around.
3. Be careful when you g**o** **ne**ar the fire.
4. We stuf**f** **our** backpacks with books.
5. With great streng**th** **ree**l in the fish.
6. The ca**t** **en**tered the room.
7. We should ba**n** **ine**ffective medicines.
8. What a cra**ze** **ro**ad-skating is!

Page 37; What's the Letter?

Sample answers are given. There might be other answers too.

1. **P**ACK **P**ECK 2. **R**ING **R**OLL
3. **B**IRD **B**OND 4. POLE **P**AIN
5. S**I**CK **S**ACK 6. T**I**RE **T**AME

Page 38; Count and Match

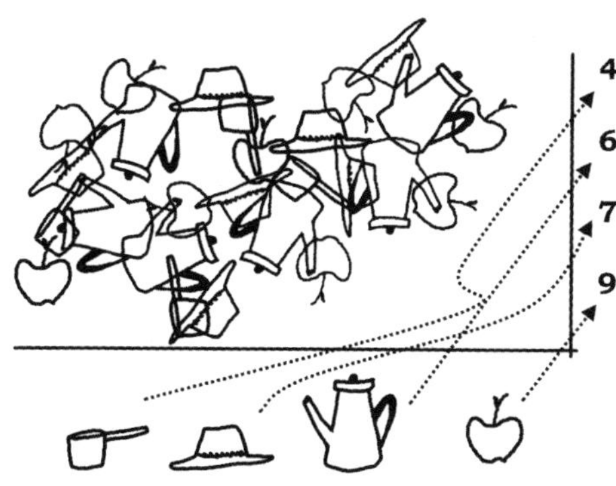

Page 39; Number the Hive

Page 40; Faded Words

Oranges, Summer, Ice Cream, Holiday, Swimming, Summer

Page 40; Words in a Circle

1. Mom/mum, peep, pop, blob, roar

Page 41; Crossword

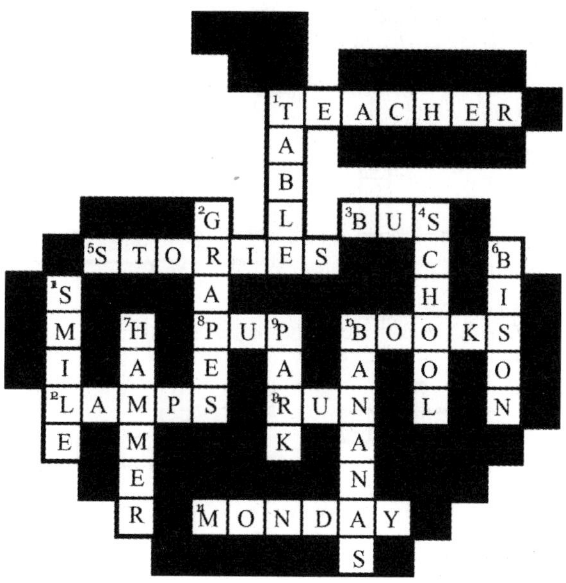

Page 42; Magician's Maze

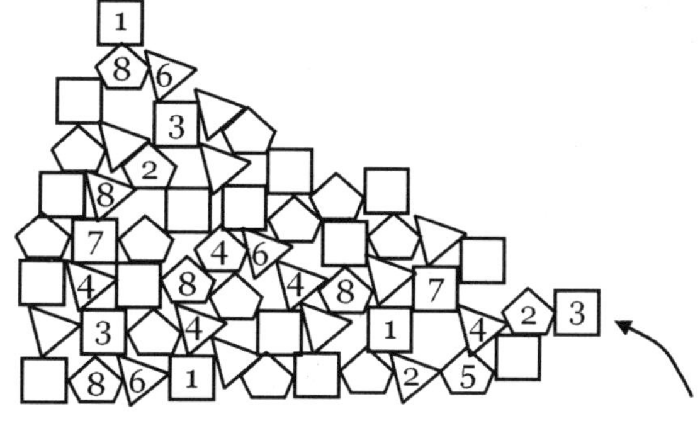

Page 43; Match the Sounds

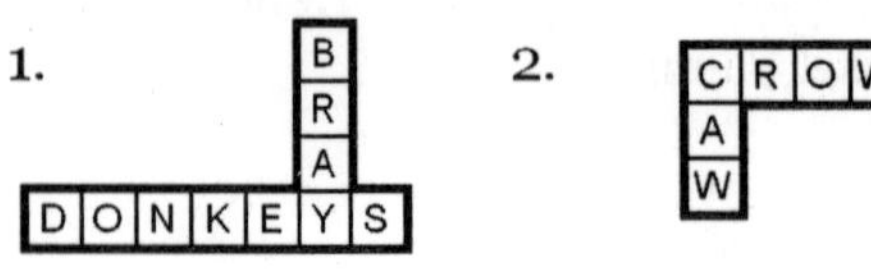

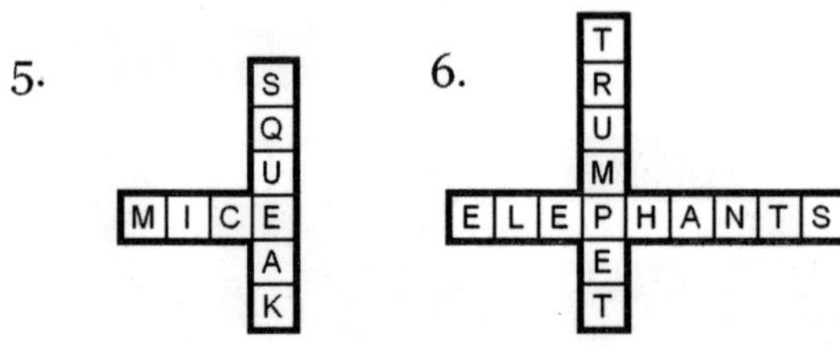

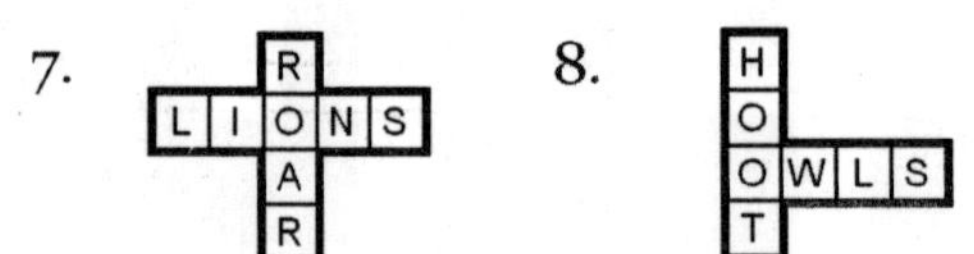

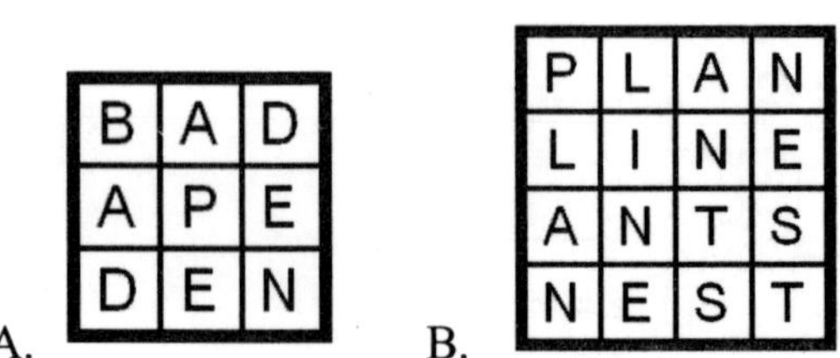

Page 44; Single Word Squares

A.

B	A	D
A	P	E
D	E	N

B.

P	L	A	N
L	I	N	E
A	N	T	S
N	E	S	T

Page 45; Lost Pictures

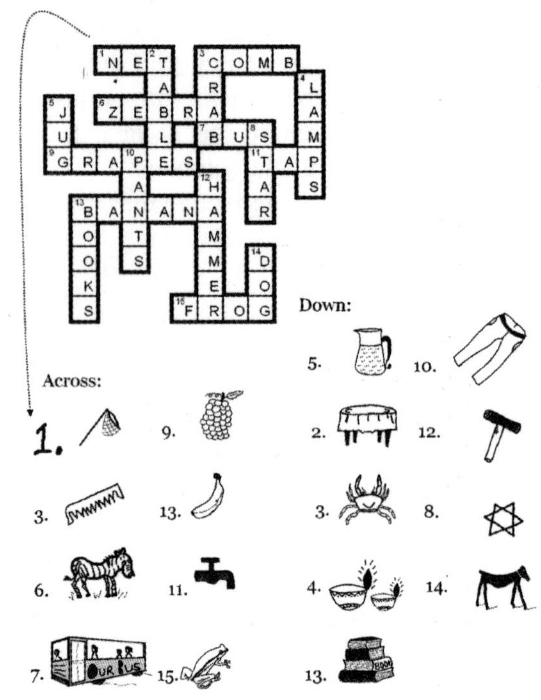

Across:

1. 9. 3. 13. 6. 11. 7. 15.

Down:

5. 10. 2. 12. 3. 8. 4. 14. 13.